Contents

Prefix

The purpose of this book is to give a house husband's perspective on raising Smalls. This may well be similar to a house wife's perspective, I do not know, I am not a house wife, but I suspect there are differences.

What it is not intended to be, is a guide to best practice, although things may be learnt for good or ill. I am not medically or psychologically trained (although I might be psychologically drained). This book is merely my own observations, based on the experience of raising three Smalls, dealing mainly with the most arduous part of the process: from birth to the successful transition out of nappies and onto the toilet.

The main character in this book is Small. Small is a general term used for a child, be it baby, toddler or older. Small may be male or female but for the purposes of this book I have used the masculine. This is not meant to be in any way sexist, it is simply that I have three boys and no girls so if I chose to refer in the feminine I would invariably makes mistakes and start to refer in the masculine. I do not believe there are any material differences between the sexes as far as they relate to this book. But I could be wrong.

Whilst this book can be read from cover to cover it has been structured as an A-Z so that it can be easily dipped in and out of. As a result there is some degree of cross referencing where some of the subject headings overlap. For instance, doidens are referred to in various subject headings but only explained under 'Doidens'. [It will make more sense once you start reading.]

I have battled with the tone of this book, most notably with my wife. She felt the first draft to be unduly harsh and critical of her perfect Smalls and that it did not reflect the true relationship of love and joy I have with them. Perhaps the main reason for this is that I am a man and she is a woman. I think it is well documented that men have difficulty in expressing their feelings and hide them behind witticisms that are often not appreciated by our female counterparts.

I therefore need to express at the beginning that whilst I would hope that women will read and enjoy this book, it has been written by a man for men. You may find some sections overly harsh and seemingly critical of Small. These are not intended as an attack on Small, they are merely a detached, clinical observation on what they are really like.

Intro

There was never any plan for me to become a house husband. When Small was first picked up on the radar my wife and I both assumed, independently of each other, that she would leave work to bring him up. That is how our parents had done things and we both turned out all right [apart from using tired old phrases like that one].

For the first few months of the pregnancy it was easy to carry on with normal life, a veil of self-imposed ignorance shrouding the changes that were to befall us. It was easy to pretend that nothing was happening.

For obvious reasons, reality began to tell on my wife first. She was starting to be constantly reminded that change had already begun and that we would have to make a start on adjusting. Like it or not, our lives were about to be transformed.

The closer we drew to Small's arrival the more frantic the efforts to get ready became. Pre-natal classes were leaving us in little doubt that if everything was not sorted out before delivery day, then it would not be sorted out at all. The third bedroom was converted from an office into a nursery and the second bedroom into an office/bedroom. Baby equipment was purchased ready for Small's arrival, his drawers were stuffed with new born clothes and a stack of nappies was placed in the corner in the hopes that we would know what to do with them when the time came. Hospital bags were packed and repacked and the car was kept permanently topped up with fuel. We were ready!

Small wasn't. He was far too comfortable where he was. Two weeks after his due date he had to be induced to step (splurge) into the light.

During the first few days, time warped. Everything was so different and alien that time stretched out, each day lasting a week. That was partly due to the mind working overtime, fuelled by a fear induced adrenaline rush; partly because there were so many things to be done and partly because we were awake for more hours than was healthy.

We made it through that initial panic and slid rapidly down the learning curve. Fortunately most of the tasks relating to Small, although new and alien, were repetitive and with each successfully completed task came greater confidence and competence.

But the thing we had shied away from, the elephant in the room, was that we would never cope financial if my wife gave up her job. With only two month of maternity leave left we began to realise that if we wanted to have a parent as a full time carer, that parent was going to have to be me. I had left my career as a solicitor to become a budding horticulturalist [sorry] 18 months earlier, taking a big salary hit at the time. We had absorbed that and the subsequent drop down to zero income could be managed, just.

So, my life of getting up at 7:00 am to be at the plant nursery by 8:00 am and then home by 5:00 pm five days a week was about to change to being at the home nursery 24/7. My life of taking little cuttings and putting them in a plastic bag was to change to one of taking little poopy nappies and putting them in a plastic bag. In short, my life of nurturing plants would become one of nurturing Smalls, only the consequences of not feeding or watering them properly were much higher. And plants, on the whole, were much quieter.

The role of the house husband is exactly the same as the role of the house wife. I found it to be a career that was stagnant from the outset. There were no opportunities for progression, defined by increased money and status. I could not excel because, whilst keeping Small physically and emotionally healthy and our home clean and tidy took an exceptional amount of work, it was the minimum that was expected of me. I was never going to be told by my boss or a member of my team that I was good at my job and nobody was going to come seeking my advice. As a job, it was never going to get better: looking after Smalls and a home is low-status, poorly rewarded and self-esteem sapping.

I can understand that from the position of being sat chained to a desk with an overbearing boss demanding to know why x, y and z have not been done, it is easy to think that being a house husband is an easy job; it is not.

True, the practical aspects of parenting – play, meals, baths and bedtimes – soon became routine, even if some of them were battle routines. Also, the basics of keeping house were not difficult, again, once routines had been established. What *was* incredibly demanding was dealing with the tedium: much of house husbanding was boring. Hours of boredom stretching from when it was still cold and dark through to when it was cold and dark again. And there was always a strong possibility that I would also be up in the middle of the cold and dark at least once.

In addition, there was little time to myself; no time for mulling over my emails (not that anyone was sending me them anymore), or surfing the web, or popping out for a run or a bike ride. There was no getting out of bed into a refreshing shower and a leisurely breakfast before work. I lived and slept in the workplace.

Then there were the hours. This was no 40 hour week. [I mistyped the last sentence when drafting and put 'jour' instead of 'hour', meaning 'day' in French. A 40 *day* week is probably about right.] Often up before the dawn, I moved from task to task whilst juggling the demands of Small for all the hours he was awake. When he slept I cracked on with the tasks I couldn't manage with him awake. If I was very lucky I sometimes got to collapse in front of the television for an hour before dragging myself off to bed for a couple of hours sleep before Small politely asked for my attention again.

On top of that, the job never really ended. Even when my wife was home, I was still at the coalface, still changing half the nappies and cooking half the meals, and still very much with Small. Weekends were like weekdays, but with help and adult company. And holidays were like weekends but in an unfamiliar place where nothing was where it should have been and everything was harder as a result. The job was relentless.

That's the bad news. The good news is that being a house husband is a huge privilege. There are not many men that get a chance to take on this emotionally extending opportunity. For instance, having worked in a plant nursery, standing all day for hours at a time taking cuttings from the same type of plant in the same greenhouse, on my own, I thought I knew a bit about patience and dealing with my own thoughts but I was wrong. Being a house husband has expanded my capacity enormously.

Nurturing Small has also given me a much greater insight into the power of looking at things from the other person's perspective. It was something I had to learn otherwise I would have suffered a lot more battle damage. Once I was able to master seeing things from another hilltop I found that most conflicts could be resolved, not just with Small but generally.

And despite the drudgery and the sleep deprivation, being with Small was a joy. One moment of Small induced happiness and pride swings the balance. A Small giggle weighs as much as a dozen sleepless nights. Eating toast with Small in a fort built out of chairs and blankets, guarded by ranks of soft toys is infinitely more rewarding than being sat in front of a computer in an office doing something that means nothing to anyone much. Seeing a happy smiling Small is the greatest feedback you can get, far more meaningful than a quickly rattled off email thanking you for your work.

More than anything, I believe a strong bond has grown between my Smalls and me that would have been weaker if I had not been at home to help their little feet find their way. Above all, I know in every fibre of my being that I will never regret being a house husband: I will not lie on my deathbed lamenting that I spent too little time with my sons when they were Smalls.

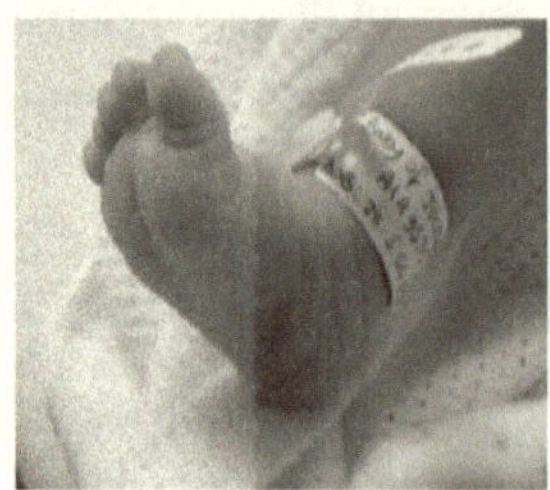

Afternoon Nap

This was something I had to give up. However, once I managed to get *Small* to have an afternoon nap it provided me with a precious hour or, if I was really lucky, two in which to double my pace and crack on with all the chores that I hadn't managed to get to because of Small.

It was really worthwhile getting Small into a regular afternoon sleeping pattern. Knowing I had 'free' time in the afternoon enabled me to relax into the hours lost playing with Small without constantly worrying about the things I was not getting done.

Problems arose with the advent of a second Small. There was no obvious benefit to having only one Small asleep so I had to work hard to establish a joint sleep routine, otherwise the Smalls formed a tag team against me.

The more Smalls you have the greater the problem becomes: statistically, your chances of free time vanish towards zero as the number of Smalls increase. Indeed, we were unlucky with Small 3, who didn't sleep in the day at all. I could count on one hand the number of times Small 3 ever slept in the day. On the positive side he was a sound sleeper at night (but always wakes between 5:00 am and 6:00 am, summer or winter). He just doesn't seem to need as much sleep as Smalls 1 & 2 did.

Baby Monitor

Most people, even those who have previously not had to venture anywhere near babies, will know what a baby monitor is. It is a trap to catch unwary, sleep deprived parents moaning about the house guests listening on the other end. It is usually obvious when this has happened because the atmosphere becomes cold enough to crack and the guests suddenly find some reason to return home. This is awkward and can mean some effort is going to have to be expended re-building relationships down the line but has the immediate benefit of relieving the stress and tension levels in the house.

Another use for the baby monitor is to listen in on Small to make sure he is okay. Some more expensive models also have a visual relay so that you can watch Small sleep. It is almost as entertaining as watching the washing machine; but not quite.

For new parents in particular, baby monitors offer reassurance that all is well with Small without the need to sneak into his room every five minutes to check he is still breathing. Of course, to hear his breathing the volume has to be cranked up to full, which is enough to burst eardrums when Small wakes up, unhappy.

If Small *is* unhappy the baby monitor becomes redundant: a Small's scream can cut through reinforced concrete. Sound proofing will prove no barrier. There is something in the pitch, modulation or intensity of a Small's cry that will cleave through everything in its path and stimulate every activating hormone a parent possesses to drag them into action, no matter how tired they are or how hard they are trying to ignore it.

Personally I found the baby monitor extremely useful if I was working in the garden whilst Small was having an afternoon nap. It meant I didn't have to keep going into the house to see if Small was awake yet, which not only used up valuable non-Small time but also ran the risk of waking him prematurely.

By the time Small 3 arrived our baby monitor had died after years of good service (and two relationship rebuilds). Fortunately by then we were confident enough to cope without it so we avoided the expense of replacing it. And there was no chance of working in the garden anyway because the other two Smalls were awake.

Bathing

It was a daunting prospect having to bathe Small for the first time. Having spent some time reading the advice on how to do it, it seemed that I needed a shed load of equipment and had a hundred things to remember if I didn't want to ruin the experience for Small and myself.

The recommended equipment that I needed, laid out ready to hand was:

- Cotton wool balls.
- Sponge or flannel.
- Mild, liquid baby cleanser [the cleanser was liquid, not the baby].
- Posset cloth (see separate listing) because Small was a boy and had a tendency to wee when his nappy came off and he felt the fresh air on his skin.
- Bath thermometer for testing the water temperature. Apparently I could have used my elbow, in which case the water should have felt neither hot nor cold, just wet, but seeing as the recommended bath temperature was between 37 & 38°c I felt there wasn't a lot of room for error and I didn't want to be responsible for either freezing or scalding Small.
- Clean, dry towel. [Hooded towels were best for wrapping up Small from top to toe.] It was recommended to have a spare towel ready in case Small spontaneously wee'd when being removed from the warm water. [Like grown men, boys are prone to weeing whenever their bits have a change of environment.]
- Clean nappy and clothes.
- Warm blanket to wrap my clothed Small in to bring him back up to sustainable living temperature. Although it was advised not to keep him in it for too long in case he became too hot.

To ensure that everything went smoothly I enlisted the assistance of my wife, so that she could to pass me equipment when I call for it, surgeon like, as

I concentrated on the tricky operation before me.

Once I had the recommended equipment laid out and my assistant standing ready, I had to ensure the environment was suitable for a naked, wet Small. That meant making sure the room was at the recommended temperature of 24°c, that all the windows were closed and there were no draughts.

The final part of preparation was to fill the bath. Whilst the 'bath' could have been a sink or the actual bath we had decided to use a baby bath; basically a suitably sized plastic tub that sits in the big bath, on the floor, on a cupboard or in its own stand. We used it in Small's room, on top of the chest of drawers where he had his nappy changed. The problem was how to fill it, which I overcame by filling it in the bath and then carrying it through to the nursery. The downside was that the filled bath was quite heavy and had a tendency to slop water on the carpet and the <u>doidens</u> (see separate listing), if they were underfoot, which they were.

With everything in place I took a deep breath and began.

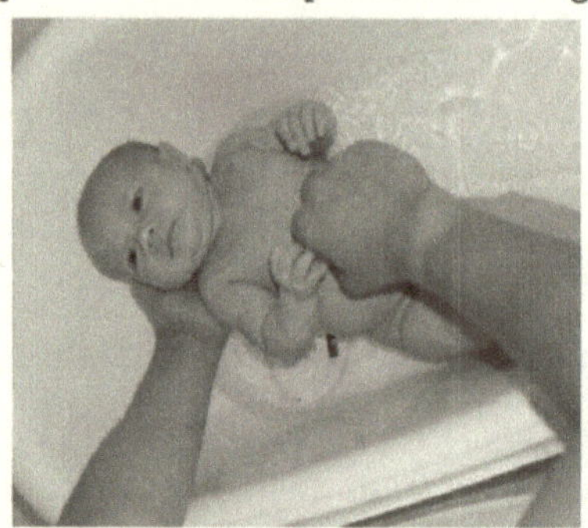

The actual process of bathing took no time at all and was completely disproportionate to the time involved in preparing for the event. This proved to be typical of any task to be undertaken with Small. It was highly labour intensive and totally inefficient. It is why I was busy dawn to dusk but never seemed to have achieve anything much at all. I began to realise that the sooner I came to terms with this fundamental fact the less stressed I would become.

I now had a clean Small, happily bundled in a warm blanket but I was not quite finished; I still had to complete the after bath process:

- First, I had to set about trying to bring the temperature of the room back down to the 16-20°c recommended for sleeping. According to the advice I had to be careful not to open any windows though, in case it caused a draught.

- Second, the bath needed to be emptied, preferably without adding to the puddles or drowning any more doidens.

- Finally, all the other mess I had created had to be tidied up. This involved binning the old nappy and used cotton wool, putting away the baby cleanser and stuffing dirty clothes and any wee soaked posset clothes and towels in the wash basket.

In the first few weeks of looking after Small there was a tendency to wash everything after one use, whether it needed it or not. For instance, even if a towel had not been weed on it was put straight in the wash. After weeks of constant washing I became more discerning.

Similarly, once I had been through the bathing process a few times it became much less fraught and more streamlined. I learnt from Small what he liked and didn't like and I was able to take pleasure in his enjoyment of the water. He gave his first proper giggles and non-wind induced smiles whilst in the bath. And we both smiled and giggled over his wind induced blurbations [not a word but it should be] in the bath. As a result, whilst the preparation and operational functions of bathing become faster, the total time spent bathing remained the same; we both just got a lot more out of it.

A few weeks down the line bathing became part of the going to sleep routine. The bathing process is sleep inducing and acted as a trigger as part of a regular sleep routine. The routine also included cuddling, rocking, reading and gentle 'FOR THE LOVE OF GOD PLEASE PUT MY SMALL TO SLEEP' music.

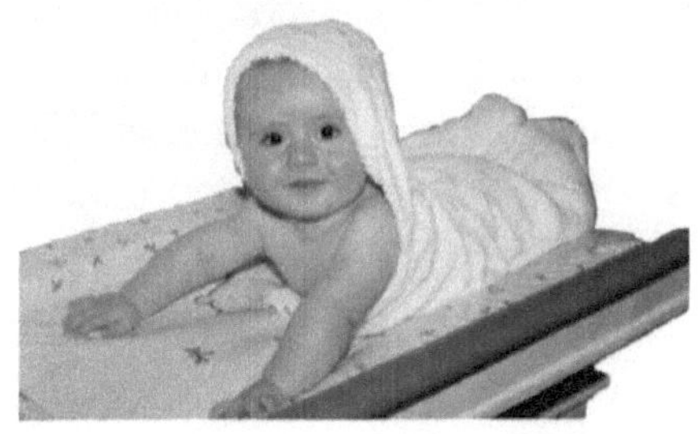

Battle of Wills

Never start a battle of wills with Small, believe me, you will lose. Male readers need only extrapolate the theory as it relates to women: giving in sooner means having to say sorry fewer times (but never less than five). Flowers also help – although maybe not with Small.

For example, if I started saying things like, "You'll not leave this table until you finish your food!" I soon found myself pleading, "Please, just eat one mouthful!" just to save face. You see, the advice I had been given was that if I lost, Small would never forget and would know that all he had to do was hold out long enough and I would crack: Small 1 Daddy 0.

I discovered the reality was that if Small didn't want to eat he wouldn't. *He* didn't ask for food. *He'd* be ready for food in five minutes time when I'd just cleared it all away.

It was tempting to elaborate and give him adult thoughts, like, "Why should I stick to your schedule?" and "You are not the boss of me!" but that would have been to demonise him. Despite what I thought, Small was not a demon, he was just totally self-centred at this stage (see The Centre of the Universe).

The positive side of this was that any idea of a score board was meaningless. That thought was actually slightly egotistic: he was not chalking up a victory over me because I did not exist, except to provide things for him, ergo; there was no victory, I had just finally got around to providing him with the thing he required, i.e. putting him back doing what he was enjoying before *I* decided he needed food.

He would also not remember all the battles, providing he got what he wanted in the end, which invariably was the case. He was doing what we should all do but cannot because life is too pressured and demanding: he was living in the moment. He was not wasting his present remembering the past (those glorious days before Small – how did I fritter away all that free time, I'm just too tired to remember) or worrying about the future (how am I ever going to get a job again with a brain like mush?), he was living in the now. So, I decided not to compound my stress by worrying that I was scarring Small with my outbursts every time the pressure got too much. I was not. [Or at least I hope not. We'll find out in a few years!] He, at least, was not keeping a tally.

Birthday Parties

This is one area that did not fall into my domain as house husband, except in so far as the leg work was concerned. Left to me, birthday parties would not exist. If they did they would be very small affairs, catered for and organised by a third party.

My wife instinctively took over arrangement for the party. She organised everything from party guests to games and music. I stayed in the background making suitable noises and completing errands when necessary. I did not suggest that, perhaps, Small was a bit too young and would not really understand what was going on. It would have been dangerous to articulate that Small might not be happy about all these people invading his space. It would have been disastrous to point out that the afternoon was the time most Smalls are grouchy and thinking about a nap.

The point I quickly managed to wrap my head around was that birthday parties, at least for the very young Small, are not being held for Small but for the parents (ok, let's face it, the mother – there, it's been said, judge me if you must). It is a once a year opportunity to show off how brilliant their Small is and, by reflection, how great they are at being a parent.

Because humans are genetically competitive, even if passively (if we weren't we would not have been the ones to survive), there was an inevitably element of making sure Small's birthday party was better than anyone else's: more balloons, better games, bigger prizes, a more sumptuous spread of food, trendier music, a hand crafted cake in the shape of Small's favourite thing and more elaborate gift bags.

The outcome was hyper tense and exhausted parents and a lot of over wrought Smalls that had had every sense pounded and really just need their afternoon nap. There were tears all round but as the organisers we had to keep ours in until all the guests had gone.

Over a number of years we developed the following party rules and even tried to follow them:

- The number of guests should be no more than one for each year old Small is.

- Not to over-elaborate. To keep things simple. Smalls like to shout, smash things, throw things and eat sweet sticky things, not necessarily in that order. A circle of Smalls with a pile of doughnuts in the middle might be the perfect party.

- If it was affordable, to go to a third party. There are plenty of activity centres/leisure centres out there that run organised parties. If it all went wrong we could blame them.

- If a parent tried to drop off their 1-2 year old and disappear, then to turn them away at the door, Small and all. They knew their Small better than we did and there would be a reason they needed 'to do some urgent shopping'.

- When Small was at pre-school or greater age to be aware of class politics. It was vital that Small's main rival was not inadvertently invited. Certainly never to invite the whole class, there was always a trouble maker and you only needed one to wreak havoc.

- When Small was old enough, to ask him to come up with a guest list. When he failed to list someone who we thought was a close friend we learnt to query this but if Small said no, then it was no. Although we did have to endure some awkward conversations and put up with some judging looks in the school queue.

- To encourage Small out of parties as soon as possible. Once their value assessment skills had kicked in, to suggest an extra present up to the cost of the party – it hasn't let us down yet (although they do try to sneak in a sleep over and a cinema trip with a couple of close friends).

- Finally, to remember that we were not there to enjoy the party. Our job was to make sure it ran as smoothly as possible whilst looking calm and relaxed, which was a bit like juggling red hot rocks with smiles on our faces.

Bottles

The bottles in my life became plastic with a teat stuck in the top rather than glass with a slice of lime or a cork stuck in the top.

Other than the obvious feeding using the bottles, one of my most sacred duties was to sterilise them.

In the early days of having a Small I had a tendency to sterilise everything as much as possible. This was a natural response to having something perfect in my home environment that I did not want to be responsible for damaging. I was aware of the millions of micro things on any given surface waiting with the express purpose of killing Small, so I defended Small by killing the millions of micro things.

After a while it slowly sank in that I couldn't stop germs getting to Small and that, if I could, he would never build any immunity to them. Therefore my manic efforts to keep everything surgically spotless diminished back to normal levels of clean. Except in one area – bottles. These were going to be stuck directly into Small's mouth and any germs there in or there on would have direct access to Small's inner most workings. They need to be sterilised.

Before sterilising, the bottles needed to be cleaned in hot soapy water. Because milk, whether formula or breast, is fatty, it clings to the bottle and the teat, therefore the advice given at our antenatal classes was to use something abrasive to scrub them. I don't think the class leader appreciated my suggestion that perhaps I could get my mother-in-law to lick them clean.

Once cleaned there were three sterilisation options; a chemical soak, boiling them in a pan or steaming them in a microwave. I chose the latter because it seemed the easiest and the quickest method. I had to buy the kit but it was not massively expensive compared to a lot of the crap I had already bought and proved to be much more useful than most of it.

The main skill with sterilising was not the sterilising itself, let's face it, the microwave does that, it was keeping it sterile. First, I had to make sure I opened the lid away from me, to avoid getting a face full of steam. Then, using the fiddly tongs provided, which were searingly hot from the steam, I had to complete the puzzle of inserting the teat into the bottle top without touching it, other than with the sterilised tongs. Next I had to cover the teat with the blisteringly hot lid. Then, taking the white hot bottle I had to fill it with boiled water to the desired level and screw on the top part I had preassembled. This process was then completed for the rest of the bottles.

If I touched a teat it was game over; re-sterilise and start again. Ditto if I forgot to put the tongs in the unit. Fortunately, this method was really quick so redoing the job was not too harsh a punishment.

Sterilising may be quick, fairly easy and relatively pain free but that is only true if you can find the equipment. We moved house when Small 2 was still a babe in arms. He would wake regularly at 2:00am for a feed (and kept it up until he was 2 years old). On the first night I realised we had run out of sterilised bottles. Not great planning but we had spent the whole day moving out of one property and into another.

I knew that, with great foresight, we had put the steriliser in the top of a box. I soon discovered that such foresight was rendered next to useless because we had not marked the box in any way. The boxes where all about me in the kitchen, stacked to the ceiling, but after 10 minutes of pressurised searching (it is amazing how much pressure a scream can exert at 2:00am) the bottle steamer could not be located.

Fortunately, Small quietened down in the car and remained calm as we trollied our way around the 24 hour supermarket praying that they had a steriliser in stock. He exploded again once we had our bounty back at the house but 20 minutes later all was well with the world once more (10 minutes sterilising the bottles and 10 minutes holding the bottle of boiling water under a running tap to cool it down to drinking temperature). Apart from the fact that my bank account was lighter and I now had a 2nd steriliser I didn't need.

Bouncing

Smalls like to bounce. At least mine do. I'm not sure why. For most adults it is not that pleasant a sensation and can bring on nausea.

Perhaps it is because Small's first experience of bouncing comes in the womb and whilst he is Small it is a comforting, regressive experience.

Once out of the womb I found that one of the best techniques for soothing Small was to gently bounce him with the back of his head cupped in my hand and his back lying along my inner forearm as I bicep curled him. With the addition of a gentle sway it probably replicated the motion of mum waddling, pre-birth.

Whilst it has made it to some 'needless baby contraptions' lists, my Smalls thoroughly enjoyed their baby bouncer. This is a sprung harness that hangs from a door frame that allows Small to push with his legs and bounce himself up and down. Small 1 in particular was an expert bouncer and would entertain himself for half an hour at a time.

Unless you have a double door it is wise to move away from the bouncer once Small can walk, otherwise all sorts of sideways motions come into play with the possibility of bashing into the door frame.

The next progression was to the trampoline. We leapfrogged the indoor trampoline, the type with a support handle, and went straight to a 10 foot garden trampoline with a full, inside the springs, net. At first it was used much like a giant play pen with lots of stumbly walking, crawling and rolling around. It was a nice place for Small to experiment because if he fell, he bounced.

Once bouncing was mastered there was no holding him back. He would bounce any when. The neighbours probably weren't too impressed about the 6:00 am sessions though.

I can honestly say that the trampoline has been the best value for money thing we have ever purchased for our Smalls. It provides hours of entertainment, fresh air and exercise. In fact, it gets used so hard that we are now on our fourth, each one lasting two to three years. Even so, buck per hour of entertainment, it is the cheapest thing I can think of.

Boys' Hair

This is a force of nature that cannot be tamed. Do not make the attempt, you are doomed to failure.

Breakages

These are to be expected so keep anything precious in a safe place (see <u>Safe Place</u>).

You may consider Small to be precious but you will probably find it impossible to confine him to a safe place. It is best to accept the inevitable – there may be breakages to Small. Hopefully these will only be in the form of self-healing surface damage but it is entirely possible that bones may also be broken. Hopefully this will only occur once Small has reached big and can assume some of the responsibility themselves.

Breast Feeding

As the male in the relationship, I could not do this but to show moral support I did get up and make notes. No, seriously – left or right boob was the most important thing to get right (so that on the next feed we didn't try to get Small to feed from the empty one). Other information of interest for notation was what time the feed took place and how long it lasted. This may seem strange but it enabled us to see patterns, such as shorter feeds that were taking place less regularly as Small became more efficient at drinking and his stomach capacity expanded. This was reassuring, letting us know that things were getting better, because they sure didn't feel like they were with the sleep deprivation beginning to have a cumulative effect.

It also became my role to retrieve Small from his basket or crib and put him back after the feed. This was not such a hardship, at least I could snooze whilst the feed itself was happening.

Another thing I had to master was 'the latch'. That was the mystic process of getting Small's tiny mouth to attach, limpet like, to a large engorged nipple. It seems that the main cause of parents giving up on breast feeding is not being able to achieve a good latch, which means Small cannot feed. It took a bit of experimentation but I discovered that my Small would latch if the nipple was approached from below. Starting with the nose below the nipple I would slide Small's face up, tilting his chin in below the nipple against the skin. Finally I would lever the upper jaw over the top of the nipple and apply a gentle pressure until Small got the idea of suckling and 'latched' on. Once Small had achieved the latch a couple of times it became second nature but the first time involved a lot of misses and a lot of screaming. We knew when we had finally achieved a latch because it suddenly got a whole lot quieter and the tension melted out of the room. I'm sure the neighbours were as relieved as us.

Whilst I could not breast feed I could feed breast milk. This introduced us to the wonders of expressing. This is essentially milking for humans. A pump, either manual or electric, is used to extract the milk from mum into plastic bags. This serves two purposes: firstly it stimulates milk production so that there is always a good supply for Small and secondly it provides stock milk that can be fed to Small when mum is not available. That might mean a feed in the middle of the night when mum is sleeping or in the daytime if mum is at work.

Incidentally, in my younger, child free days one of the gadgets on my wish list was a drinks fridge. One of those glass fronted mini chillers filled with wine and beer. Long before that was ever to materialise we obtained a breastmilk freezer. Actually we didn't acquire the breast milk freezer, it was just that our existing freezer started to overflow with breastmilk. You see, breastmilk can be stored in the freezer for several weeks and safely used. Providing we kept the bags labelled with the date, we had a rolling back-up supply of milk that lasted for months. The breastmilk freezer proved invaluable. Just as valuable as that drinks fridge would have been.

If mum is breast feeding and you are house husbanding there will come a time when mum is back at work and you are left with the feeding responsibility. It is highly likely that by this stage Small will be used to having a bottle from you and this will not be an issue. However, this was not the case for us. Small 1 was an avid breast man and refused to drink from a bottle, even breast milk. In the age old tradition of ostriches everywhere we stuck our heads in the sand and ignored the issue, taking the easy option of offering direct breast action.

So it was that on my first day as full time house husband I was faced with a hungry Small that refused to take a bottle. Now, I thought that once he was hungry enough he would take the bottle. No. He was (is) a stubborn little bugger. He screamed for England, and at three months his lungs had developed nicely.

There followed hours of crying, interspersed with mere mumble sobbing when the bottle was removed from his presence and all the standard calming techniques were employed (see Calming). Eventually he took the bottle, strapped to my chest in a papoose, watching television as I rocked gently sideways, back and forth from foot to foot. The bottle was drained in less than a minute.

Although perhaps I had the easier time. At least I was coping in the privacy of my own home. Whilst at work, every time it would have been time to feed Small, my wife had to go to an especially dedicated room to express her milk into a plastic bag. Her not too politically correct work colleagues had put up a sign in the blacked out window - 'Milking Shed'.

Bruises, Cuts and Scrapes

I took infinite care with our Small, never allowing him to come into contact with sharp objects or hard surfaces. I was largely successful, until he started crawling. Even then, with due diligence, I managed to prevent all injuries. But, after all my care and attention, Small eventually made it onto his feet and the real trouble began. You see, despite all my diligence and love and attention, Small had no regard for his own safety whatsoever. In fact, the opposite seemed to be the case. Small appeared to come with a built in homing mechanism that sought out the most lethal things in his immediate environment. No matter how many 'safe' toys and distractions were placed about Small, he will unerringly headed towards the one thing that would do him harm.

Similarly, Small seemed to have something akin to a magnet in his head. This was a device with special properties that not only attracted metal but any hard surface, in particular patios and the corners of tables.

No matter how many times I had cut myself my first sight of Small's blood was quite devastating. It was only then that I came to the realisation that this red stuff should have been on the inside and didn't have any place being outside. It was an abomination that it should be leaking out of my perfect child. I felt terrible that I hadn't managed to keep Small fully intact and that his injury was all my fault.

From some way down the tracks I can now say that the feelings were somewhat akin to having a new pair of jeans. The first time they get a stain it is a disaster of biblical proportions but with each new stain and blemish the hurt becomes less and less until they are just an old pair of jeans. It is much the same with Smalls.

Small had received his first cut simply because he had reached that age, i.e. the actively mobile, independent stage. From there on, cuts and bumps became pretty frequent and there was little I could do to prevent them. The good news was that wounds healed amazingly quickly on Small. I soon moved from guilt over the blemishes to saying, "Well of course he has a bruise on his forehead – he is a child!"

Calming

When the screaming starts and you have been through the checklist under <u>crying</u> (see separate listing) and nothing appears out of place how do you calm the situation down?

Personally I always found that a dark room, a familiar blanket and some soothing music helped considerably. The trouble was, the screaming Small normally spoilt it, so I also had to find some way of calming him down.

Through frantic trial and error I found the following helped:

- Cradling Small in my arms and swinging from side to side, rotating at the hips.
- Cradling Small in my arms and rocking sideways from foot to foot, extending up onto toes for more vigorous rocking.
- Gentle bouncing – with Small's head cupped in my hand, his back along my forearm, his feet either side of my upper arm I would bicep curl him up and down. If necessary I would add a gentle sway from side to side.

Extreme situations called for all three at once.

In an attempt to reduce the manual labour involved, for Small 3 we purchased a mechanical swing cradle/seat. Powered by batteries, it rocked Small back and forth or sideways, depending on how it was configured, keeping him soothed whilst I could get on with something else. It was expensive and only of use for about 6 months before he became too heavy for it but it was invaluable: it provided 20 minutes first thing each morning to get vital supplies of coffee on board and to drag myself awake enough to cope. After the six months it was still in perfect condition (even the original batteries still going) and we sold it to recoup half the purchase price so we considered it money well spent.

When none of the above techniques were having any effect more drastic measures were required:

- Going for a walk with Small in the backpack or in the pushchair.

- Going out with Small on the back of the bicycle.
- Going for a drive in the car.

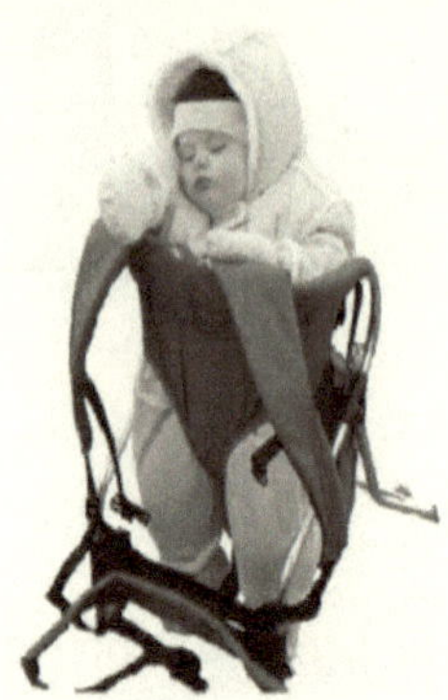

The first two options were rather too public on the occasions that Small decided not to calm down. The bicycle was a particularly bad option when that occurred because it looked like I was forcing Small to do something he really didn't want to. So, after a couple of failures I dropped it in case the local authorities decided to pay a friendly visit.

When you have more than one Small, things can get tricky. Invariably, when I paid attention to one Small, by rocking for instance, the other would start to play up. My number one solution was therefore to do something that would calm Small 1 whilst entertain Small 2. This meant a tour around the town in the tandem buggy.

The tandem buggy was like a juggernaut. With two Smalls on board it weighed in at 50kg. That was quite a bit of weight to push around a town made up of 10% gradient hills. It was hard on the legs, shoulders and lungs on the ups and put a strain on the hamstrings on the downs because there were no brakes to mitigate the inexorable drag of gravity.

In addition to the pushing was the lifting. Due to the buggy's design, the heaviest of the Smalls needed to sit up front, putting most weight at the end furthest from the pivot point when it came to levering the front wheels up to mount kerbs. This was exacerbated by the very short extension handle which providing no leverage when pushing down on it to raise the front wheel. The local authority had not thought hard about wheelchairs and pushchairs so there were few breaks in the kerbs meaning a fair weight training session by the time a circuit of the town was completed.

Usually both Smalls dropped off to sleep. However, there was no point going back to the house because I couldn't get the tandem inside without collapsing it. That would mean taking the Smalls out, which would wake one or both up. So I ended up walking around for an hour, up and down the hills with my 50 kg miniature juggernaut. Providing it wasn't chucking down with rain it was quite pleasant, it kept me fit and provided a quiet time once a day. But it was dicey when icy.

Climbing

Climbing follows on from crawling, often preceding walking. It was not long after dragging himself to his feet by the sofa that Small hauled himself *onto* the sofa. From there it was a short crawl and scramble to the top of the sofa back from where there would have been a swift plunge to the floor. Fortunately our sofa backed up against the window but that meant that the windowsill beckoned. Now was the time to make sure windows were not left open.

Our Smalls spent a lot of time on the windowsill, both inside and out. You see, it didn't take long for Small to master opening the window and we had no keys to lock it. Fortunately it was only a short drop to the front garden and we had cushioned it with gravel. [No Smalls were injured in the writing of this paragraph.] I think Small learnt the trick of standing on the outside windowsill from the doidens (see <u>Doidens</u>). He didn't bark at everyone that walked past though.

Small could also often be found on the cabinet or scaling the indoor clothes airer. It soon became clear that we had better not accidentally leave the loft ladder down.

The thing Small most liked to climb was the stairs. Gates at the top and bottom became essential until Small was stable on his feet and could be trusted to scoot down the stairs on his bum.

Climbing proved to be an ongoing activity and Small soon graduated to walls and trees. This is traditionally when breakages are most likely to occur: when Small has mastered climbing (or thinks he has) but not learnt the fear of consequences.

When it comes to climbing, I found that the best place for Small was in a soft play area or the local park. Here I had three choices:

- Follow Small around and help him over every obstacle.
- Sit on a bench and watch, letting Small have free roam so he could hone his skills, meanwhile biting my fingernails to the quick.
- Look the other way and hope for the best.

Prior to our own Smalls I remember visiting my brother-in-law and his family. My nephew, a little over two at the time, was at the top of a climbing frame and was about to attempt to swing himself over the top so he could climb down the other side. I was aghast, thinking only of the consequences of falling and positioned myself underneath him, ready to catch. 'Be careful,' I said, 'you might fall.' He responded with, 'But I might not.' And threw his leg over and scrambled down the other side.

It was a good philosophy and one that all Smalls live by. It always springs to mind every time I need to make a frightening decision.

Clothes

I tended to dress Small in the same way I dress myself; in whatever is most comfortable and practical. In Small terms, at least for the first few months, that meant a vest and a sleep suit. These garments have minimal bulk and few seams, thus providing comfortable lying, and they also allow easy access for nappy changes, once the poppers have been mastered.

My experience was that mothers seem to suffer from a need to dress their Smalls like mini adults. True, Small can look cute but it is all extremely expensive and it is both less comfortable and practical. For example, at the weekly weighing session (see <u>Targets</u>) I had been known to strip my Small, have him weighed and re-dressed before other parents have managed to undress their designer clad Small.

Whilst, in relation to income, clothes these days are not as expensive as they once were, thanks to the exploitation of the developing world, the cost still mounts up. It was frustrating that Small out grew his clothes every few months; weeks in the early days. As a result we were left with a huge bundle of clothes that had been worn twice and a lot that had never been worn at all. These could have been sold but nobody wanted second hand clothes for their precious new perfect Small. For the same reason, even giving them away proved difficult.

In the hopes of another Small we boxed the clothes up and put them in the loft. The important factor here, though, was that it had to be another Small of the same sex. There were few items that were unisex. Even the sleep suits were stereotypical blues. In hindsight we should have bought neutral colours and clothes that were as non-gender specific as possible.

You can imagine my joy when first Small 2 and then Small 3 was pronounced as a boy. By the end, maximum value had been squeezed out of most of the clothes, although I begrudged the wear left in some (but not enough to contemplate a Small 4).

Incidentally, the same non gender specific rule could apply to the nursery: it is all very well decorating it in pink and purple for a female Small but what happens when male Small 2 arrives? Either there is all the hassle and expense of redecorating or he ends up with an unexplained complex later in life.

Collections

Many humans have a built in need to collect things that are interesting or seem important because they remind us of important events. A simple form is a collection of photographs. In the past many people had, or still have, boxes and album full of snapshots of their lives. Nowadays there are even greater collections but they take up little room because they are digital. If I printed all the photographs on my computer I'm certain they would fill a small room.

A large chunk of my loft is filled with much smaller collections. Sadly, being physical they take up a much larger space. These are Smalls' collections: either a Small collected them or they are collections relating to the things Smalls have achieved.

However, the most grisly collection is held in a small ornate box hidden at the back of a drawer. If you happened to be rummaging in my drawers and discovered it you would be filled with revulsion. The first grisly thing in the box is the clip from Small 1's umbilical cord that stopped the blood leaking out after it was cut. It still has some air dried, desiccated cord attached. Next comes a curl from his first haircut, tied with a piece of ribbon (Small never wore ribbons). Then there is a gruesome collection of little teeth, some with dried blood still staining then. Why, oh why, oh why? When Small is big he will certainly not appreciate them.

At least the body parts mean something and the events can be remembered. Later there will be a collection of paper item: birthday cards, first writing (meaningless squiggles), colouring, drawing, star charts for being good, first work at pre-school, well done stickers from the dentist, second writing, more star charts, another thick wedge of colouring (Small can get through a colouring book in minutes – it's easy when you just scribble a knot of blue crayon on each page), progress books from preschool, writing with shapes that could vaguely be actual letters, colouring using more than one colour...

Then there is a cot, a crib a moses basket, linen and blankets, first shoes, first wellies, clothes, second shoes, second wellies, rattles, rings, play mats, a travel cot, activity centres, hobby horses, Ben 10 figures, Mike the Knight figures, bags of Puffles and other soft toys, and box after box after box of

Thomas the Tank Engine trains and tracks.

It is all up there, in the loft. There is probably more than what is listed: I haven't conducted a full inventory, it's too damned scary to go up the ladder anymore.

My wife is working on getting rid of things but it is slow progress. As soon as one batch is dispatched from the house another, from slightly bigger Smalls, takes its place.

The point is, it is useless to keep this stuff. When Small is big he will not appreciate it and it will become his problem. When my parents-in-laws moved home they sent my wife a very large trunk filled with memorabilia from her childhood. Whilst it raised a few happy memories when it was first opened most of the items in it had lost any meaning, if they had ever had any, to my wife. They were more things that her mum and dad had memories of. So, the large trunk now sits in our loft because we would feel guilty if we got rid of it. [Yes, we have a very big loft.]

Crawling

It was a great moment when Small finally struggled onto all fours and flopped on his face an inch forward of where he started. It was one of the monuments of development which was duly noted for posterity and used as a bragging tool against any of Small's contemporaries that hadn't already accomplished the feat. After all those weeks and months of struggle it felt like I was finally getting somewhere: Small was on the move.

Yes, Small was on the move and the trouble began. Up until that point, Small had been demanding and noisy but I could be fairly sure that if I left him somewhere he would still be there when I came back (he wasn't a roller). Now I couldn't leave him anywhere because by the time I came back he would be gone. As a result I had to make sure there was nothing dangerous at floor level and the stair gates that had been hanging around in their box for months had to be installed pronto.

Despite any comments about over sanitising things elsewhere in the book, I now needed to keep the floors clean and free from anything potentially harmful to an inquisitive crawler that had a tendency to explore the properties of things by sticking them in his mouth. For instance, the doidens' (see Doidens) food bowls needed to be picked up after feeding (not that doiden food would have done Small much harm and it might have even be somewhat tastier than the mush he was used to).

Fortunately the doidens in the house had become fully acclimatised to Small because now he was joining them in their beds and was washing himself in their water bowl.

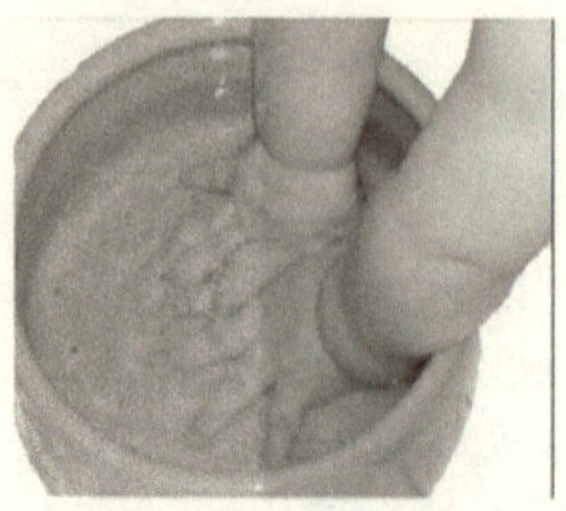

Also, having small sized doidens we have a doiden flap in the back door, which provided endless entertainment for Small and also an escape route into the garden, where all sorts of horrors awaited (see Garden).

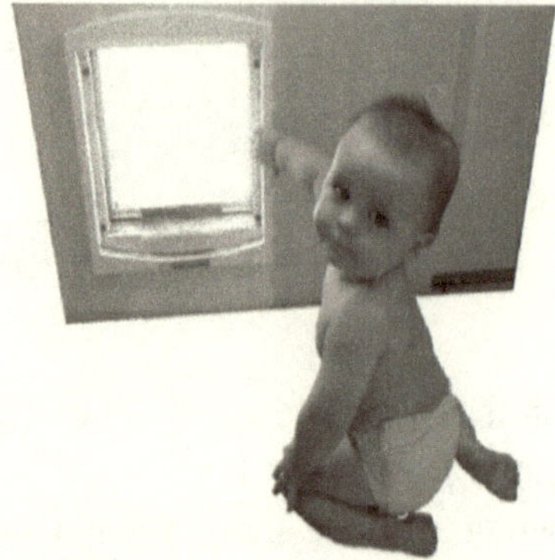

Major points of interest for a crawling Small included electrical sockets, the TV and all the junk associated with it like sound bars, dvd/blueray players, games consoles, satellite/cable boxes and all those intriguing wires. We have all heard clichéd tales of toast posted into the video recorder and I can tell you that they are true (younger reader may have to look up what a video recorder is but it was like a clunky sort of dvd or blueray player). In fact, most of the clichés you hear about living with a Small are true.

I designated a drawer at floor level for Small and then filled it with all the things he most liked to play with. This provided him with a distraction from opening everything else. Well, mostly. In fact we had two drawers for Small, one in the living room and one in the kitchen. Technically, the one in the kitchen was not his, it was filled with our motley collection of plastic tubs, but it soon became his.

We had to fit child locks to cupboards and drawers with breakables and things that could be dangerous (cleaning fluids etc.). They are still in place, even though the smallest Small is well past the random destruction phase. Destruction is much more focussed these days.

Crèche

Not long into my career as house husband I realised that if I wanted to retain some semblance of sanity, at least sanity as judged by non-Small possessed people, I needed some time away from Small. With no family back-up, our closest relative living a four hour journey away, I had to seek out other sources of relief.

After a bit of research I decided to join our local leisure centre for the sole purpose of utilising its crèche facility. The facilities for Small were excellent for all ages of Small up to school age, with soft play, lots of ride along trucks and trikes, toys and even a bouncy castle.

On joining the leisure centre I had no thought about trying to get fit but the crèche was only available whilst you were using the leisure facilities. Needless to say, I have never been so fit (or so tired) in my life.

Whilst the crèche offered me freedom, if only for a short time, it also offered Small a wonderful opportunity to intermingle with other smalls and learn new skills. I was amazed by the number of new things that Small was able to do after only a few visits. Unfortunately the new skills were not particularly helpful to me because they generally involved throwing things, climbing on things and jumping (or falling) off things. This meant that previous safe areas were no longer safe and ornaments and knickknacks had to be moved to the loft, which at that stage was relatively empty (see Collections).

Crying

There was a lot of this. I wasn't used to dealing with it but I consoled myself that it was natural and nothing to worry about.

Small cried a lot too.

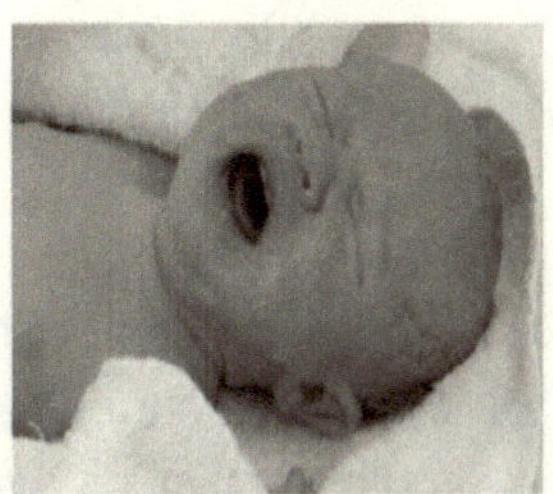

For a long time Small's only form of communication was to cry. Therefore there was a lot of crying. When Small wouldn't stop crying I told myself that he was just a very communicative child. Whilst it felt like a bad thing at the time I knew from all the stories and anecdotes I had ever heard that in a few years, once Small had fully mastered speaking, he would likely give it up as a bad lot, communicating only in monosyllables if I was lucky, if not grunts. I tried to convince myself that at that point I would look back on this incessant crying phase with some degree of fondness.

When faced with a particularly tenacious bout of crying the doidens would often hear me sobbing, "Why can't you just tell me what is wrong!" If Small had mastered spoken language he would have probably replied, "I am, you're just not bloody listening!"

Unfortunately Small wasn't going to master spoken language anytime soon so it was up to me to learn Screamish. This took practice. I had to listen to many screams. It was a slow process but eventually I picked up the subtle differences between screams and was able to determine what was wrong. During the learning process I used the following useful checklist of possible ailments:

- Hungry.
- Hot/cold.
- Dirty nappy.
- Tired.

- Bored.
- Not well.
- Generally miserable.
- Testing lungs capacity.
- Testing response rate of parent.
- Wanting to say hello because he hasn't seen you for 5 minutes (default behaviour during the hours of darkness).

As time progressed more cries evolved but I diligently stuck to my study of Screamish and began to associate different cries with different problems (a cry was always associated with a problem of some form). In an attempt to bypass this problem recognition element of the crisis resolution process I even tried to instil in Small the management ethos of 'bring me solutions not problems' but that was a complete washout.

As time progressed, the cry evolved a spin off species known as the whinge and later still the tantrum.

Cuddles

These helped enormously to ease tears and fears and to calm down tantrums and whinges. They were required frequently. Small also benefitted from cuddles. Sometimes I killed two birds with one stone by cuddling Small. Or, to mix metaphors, grasped the nettle.

Joking aside, one of the greatest joys of parenthood is to receive a full blown, genuine 'I love you mummy/daddy' hug from your Small.

Dancing

Small danced like me – feet planted firmly to the floor whilst bobbing at the knees or gently rocking left and right from foot to foot, with some rotation when feeling extremely adventurous. With both techniques the arms pumped in and out in jerky, rapid and random motions, often with fingers pointed. Note: music was not always required.

Watching Small dance was a joy because he was totally uninhibited. The dancing had to be spontaneous though. When we started asking Small 1 to dance, especially for other people, he soon learnt what embarrassment was and never want to dance again. We didn't make the same mistake with Smalls 2&3.

Doidens

Doidens covers two categories. Firstly dogs or doggies, which is what doidens are (possibly: see below) and secondly, first words.

In the vocabulary of Small 1, doidens were dogs. Possibly. It might have been the name of one of our dogs (Bronwyn) or it could have been anything furry with four legs (because cats were also doidens). Then again, it might have been a greeting (because it was often employed when a doiden was first spotted and this included mum, who wasn't furry and four legged). Alternatively it could have merely been an exclamation of surprise and delight because the bees buzzing lazily through the lavender were doidens too.

Dogs

For our purposes, here and now, we will pretend that doidens meant dogs, so that I can tell you about dogs.

Dogs are great for Smalls. Sadly Smalls are not necessarily great for dogs. The dogs will not only suffer from physical abuse, such as the pulling of hair and the poking of eyes and noses (and other more private and gruesome areas) but also the mental anguishes associated with the introduction of a new pack member. There will be the usual jockeying for hierarchical pack position. This may not be a problem if the dog knows its place is firmly at the bottom of the pile but even then it may consider that any new recruit to the pack should automatically rank below it. There will be even more of a problem if the dog is a social climber.

We had one of each variety; a Scottie who seemed to know her place but was nevertheless put out when a new pack member instantly got better privileges than her (such as eating and sleeping on demand and almost constant attention from the Pack Leader and the Lead Bitch) and a Corgi 'princess' who was constantly seeking ways to elevate her status to that of Lead Bitch. So, whilst the Scottie was mildly frustrated with the new pack members' instant high status, the Corgi's royal nose was put completely out of joint; she now had three extra rivals to climb over on her way to the top.

Small benefitted from doidens in the household because:

- doidens were fun to play with, in particular they were good to chase under the dining room table and chairs;
- Small grew up unafraid of doidens; and
- from a medical point of view, early interaction with doidens can assist the development of Smalls immune system.

There are obvious disadvantages should the physically and mentally abused doiden turn on Small, which always has to be a consideration. If you are concerned about this at all then you should seek some professional advice as the problem, or perceived problem, may be easily overcome.

Dogs as horses - *I have been asked by my Corgi to make a quick note at this point – dogs are not horses (or ponies, mules, donkeys or anything similar) and should not be ridden by Small (or to use her own words, "One is a princess, not a beast of burden. One was born to ride, not to be ridden."*

It later became apparent that doiden in Smallish wasn't a direct translation of dog or doggies after all. It was more probably an attempt at 'gentle'. Of course, doggies became doidens because every time Small approached them, fingers extended ready to probe, he was told to be gentle.

The same can be said for cats, bees and mummy.

Ironically, the doggies in the household are now referred to as gentles.

First words

Small's first words were an exciting time for both of us. Finally a stage had been reached where we were able to communicate fully. Now Small could tell me what all the tears were about. He could get his life sorted and I could bypass all that noise whilst I tried to guess what was wrong. Sadly not. Early verbal communication was extremely frustrating. What exactly did doiden mean? Small had spent months learning how to say doiden and now daddy didn't seem to know what it meant! Even with the frantic waving of arms and repeating the word several times the message didn't seem to be getting across. Needless to say, daddy wouldn't have known a doiden if it came up and bit him, which was a possibility depending on which definition was accepted.

This was particularly maddening during activities that had a high latent background tension, such as mealtimes. Already a battleground, Small now had a new weapon. Thinking myself familiar with the routine, I had set out my battle plan. I knew my goals: all food eaten – unrealistic and unobtainable; food half eaten – total victory; one spoonful smeared around the vicinity of Small's mouth – victory; nothing eaten but not too much of it ending up all over small, the high chair, the floor and me – victory. I knew small's moves and I could counter them, sometimes.

Then Small changed the game completely by throwing a direct command at me.

"DOIDEN!"

Scratching my head I wondered what he meant.

"DOIDEN!"

He must have wanted something. What?

"DOIDEN!!"

"I don't know what a doiden is."

"DOIDEN!!"

Nerves ragged I cast about – spoon! I handed over the spoon. The spoon hit the floor as, "DOIDEN!!!" reverberated from the walls. There was a lot of seemingly random pointing and vague gesturing in the general direction of the thing that was required. Drink? The drink joined the spoon.

"DOIDEN!!!!"

"I don't know what a doiden is! Why can't you just tell me?"

"DOIDEN DOIDEN!!"

Biscuit? The floor was looking quite cluttered now.

"DOIDEN!"

Totally phased I threw some idioms at the problem: discretion is the better part of valour – best to think this through and live to fight another day. I hoisted Small from the chair and he toddled happily away, gleefully throwing over his shoulder, "Doiden!"

Small was very keen on his first word and didn't particularly want to have to go through the effort of learning a second one, so I had to learn to pick up the subtle differences in pronunciation which deferred a different meaning to the same word. We have already discussed how doiden could mean many things. The second stage added tiny variations, for instance darden meant garden and daden meant daddy (possibly).

In those moments of confused communication I dearly wished that Small would develop a greater vocabulary. A few more words would have helped enormously. It was a shame he couldn't read a dictionary. What if there was a recorded one he could listen to? Or a video showing him what things were called? Was there an app that could be downloaded? I realised that was modern, lazy thinking and that it was my job to teach him the names of things. So, when I offered him a cup, I told him it was a cup or a drink or juice. Once he had mastered the sounds he would repeat it back and progress was made. [Of course, progress would have been faster if I hadn't confused him by calling the same thing a number of different names.] More words appeared and communication became less fraught. There was less frantic waving of arms and shouting because Small could start to tell me exactly what his urgent need was.

Things went well from there until somehow he picked up the word, 'why'. From that point every sentence became prefixed with, 'why'. Sometimes there was no sentence, just that word, 'why'. It drove me very close to the edge of insanity. There was no end to the use of the word. At one point I counted how many 'whys' Small 3 used in a two minute period: **27!** The worst thing was, there actually was no answer to the question 'why' that couldn't be countered with a further, "Why?". The closest I came was, "Because!" Not correct but Small learnt that once that point had been reached it was best to shut up for a minute or two.

Thankfully the whys eventually dried up. I breathed a sigh of relief at the time but a few years later I find myself complaining that Small(ish) never shows much interest in the things going on around him. Why does he never wonder about how things work or what they are there for? Sadly the answer is probably that I drove it out of him with, "Because!"

Whilst on the subject of first words, it is well known that a common first, or at least early, word is daddy. This is not because daddy is the greatest thing in Small's world, it is because it is a nice easy sound for a Small to make. Nevertheless, it is a sound that filled me with joy: my Small was finally communicating in real words and was recognising me and the efforts I had been putting in on his behalf. I was his daddy.

Later in Small's development, "Daddy," became a hammer blow to my central nervous system. Every question and every demand became prefixed with, "Daddy…" "Daddy, I'm hungry!" "Daddy, I'm thirsty!" "Daddy, I need a poo!" "Daddy, my legs are bendy!" "Daddy, why…?" Daddy was used countless times an hour and soon lost its charm.

Sometimes first words did not bear much relationship to the actual word Small was trying to master. Communication is of course a two way process and, as such, I had to master Small's language as much as he had to learn mine. In the same way that Small had to hear a word and be shown its association many times, I required the same. For instance, it took me some time to realise that 'Stidid' was Small 1's best attempt at Small 2's name. For a long time after that he was always called Stidid, which probably didn't help Small 1's language development at all.

First words are cute. In most cases they can only be interpreted by the parents and are a meaningless noise to a third party. However, Small 3 managed to articulate, "Oh God!" clearly and loudly from a very young age, a phrase he learnt from his older brothers (six and seven years older). A blaspheming one year old certainly turns heads in public.

His older brothers also taught Small 3 useful words like poo. In fact the ring tone on my phone is a rendition of the song Row, Row, Row Your

Boat… at full gusto by Small 3 using only the word poo for lyrics.

As Small developed he also came out with priceless sentences that I will never forget. One bright sunny day, when setting off for the crèche, with snacks in hand, in our super flash, Porche red, three wheeled, twin sports buggy, with the top down, Small 1 turned to Small 2 and said, "This is the life, eh Stidid!" Goodness knows where he picked up that phrase but it was perfect for the moment.

Dimmer Switches

A dimmer switch toggles on and off with a push and allows the brightness of a light to be varied. I sometimes wished my Smalls had come with a dimmer switch but that was just a dream. A wistful dream. But if there are any scientists at the forefront of genetic manipulation reading, it's a thought for the future.

In the meantime, we found dimmer switches to be very useful in any room that Small was likely to go to sleep in, e.g. our room and the nursery. A dimmer switch had two advantages over a traditional switch:

- Most obviously, it allowed the amount of light in the room to be varied. After a snatched hour or twos sleep in the blessed darkness the eruption of light from a bulb at full power was blinding, for Small, my wife and me, when Small woke demanding…something. The light on its dimmest setting was plenty.

- The toggle click on and off was easy to operate simply by leaning your shoulder on the switch, a boon when my hands were full, either with Small, an armful of junk as I moved it about the house (see Efficiency) or both.

The downside of dimmer switches was that on its lowest setting the light could sometimes appear not to be on at all during daylight. There was a tendency to leave them on as a result. Later, when the daylight faded I would notice that the light had been on all day. This was obviously a waste but the real problem was that my wife became convinced that the house was haunted.

Dopen

Dopen was the name Small 2 gave to a Winnie the Pooh teething blanket (see pic). It went with him everywhere and was a vital ingredient when going to sleep. It was a comforter.

Small 2 is not unusual in having a comforter. Many Smalls get their comfort from dummies, or pacifiers as they are known in the US. Others have a small soft toy or a rag or blanket, perhaps most famously Linus from the Peanuts cartoons.

Whatever form they take, comforters are great because they provide almost instant, well, comfort to both Small and, consequently, the parents. That is until they go missing. Then they are the worst thing in the world because Small CANNOT be comforted without his dopen.

I have lost count of the number of times our house has been frantically turned over, desperately searching for dopen. We tried having a duplicate dopen, exactly the same in every respect, for when dopen went missing. Clearly it was not exactly the same because it was never accepted.

We discovered that the important thing about dopen, as far as Small was concerned, was the label. Small wasn't brand conscious; it was literally the label. He sucked on it. The label on the copy dopen was not the same, mainly because it had not been sucked almost to the point of disintegration. We could see a disaster looming: what would happen when the label did disintegrate?

On investigation it seemed Small was not alone in his taste for labels and one company had made a similar blanket that had tens of labels of all different materials and textures all around the edge of the blanket. This was purchased and rejected. We tried weathering the label on the duplicate dopen by a process of prolonged soaking and occasional rubbing. After days of work the result when dopen was substituted by sleight of hand was a moment's hesitation, a puckered brow… and then rejection.

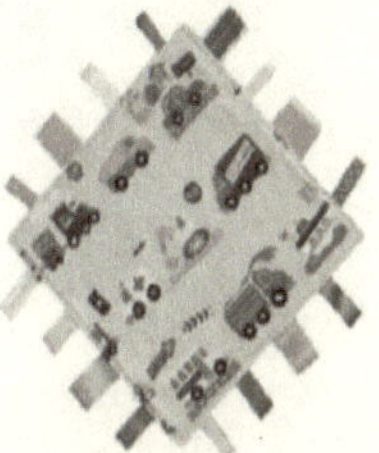

Fortunately Small 2 grew out of his dopen just before the label was completely sucked into oblivion. There was no lead out period to not wanting dopen. One night he cuddled on the blanket and champed on the label, the next he didn't. And never did again. To sentimental parents this seemed very hard on dopen, his sleep buddy for so long, but to Small he just no longer needed it. Small had no emotional tie to dopen, other than it was something he wanted - and now didn't.

In the same circumstances an adult would probably keep hold of dopen, firstly because it was something they had liked (sentiment), secondly in case they started to like it again (denial) and thirdly because it was still in good working order and it had cost money (guilt). This is why many adults have so much junk. Small had not developed sentiment, denial or guilt and happily crawled on to the next important thing in his life without looking back once.

The sudden rejection of once favourite things was displayed throughout Small's development (see Fads) but as he developed emotionally the rejected items were more likely to be shoved in the back of the cupboard rather than the bin. In many respects I find it sad how quickly Small learnt to be a hoarder but perhaps I shouldn't have moaned so much about the cost of all those things he was rejecting, seemingly on a whim. I have to remember that, to a large extent, Small learnt everything from me.

Dummies

In the US these are known as pacifiers, a name becoming more common in the UK. However, whilst a logical name, a pacifier in the UK is also a nickname for a rubber cosh, so conjures up the wrong images for me.

To use or not to use, that is the big dilemma. We all have an image of the dummy dependent 5 year old heading off to school in our heads and do not want to go there. On the other hand, when faced with a screaming Small at 2:00am, that possibility is 5 years away. In the very early days when time is extremely elastic and each day lasts a week, you might as well be talking about another lifetime.

There is no denying that a dummy can provide instant relief to Small and, by consequence, the parents. In summer, with all the windows open, it might just provide relief to the whole street. That is, until it falls out.

There is no right or wrong answer to the dilemma. Everyone has to solve it for themselves. Dummies were not used in our house because it was thought they would become like the morning coffee I had already begun to rely upon: dependency generating. Small and I would become dummy addicts. Small would grow so accustomed to sucking on his dummy that if I tried to take it away I would just end up releasing all the cries I had been plugging in for weeks in one almighty torrent. And because the dummy would provide such instant comfort, it would instinctively become the go to method to stop Small crying, probably stopping me going through the checklist of what might actually be wrong with Small (see Crying).

So, we did not use dummies. But we still ended up with Smalls suffering from a dopen dependency (see Dopen), which was really exactly the same thing. The advantage of a dopen, though, was that seeing a Small cuddling a soft toy/blanket brings a gleam of merriment to most peoples' eyes whereas seeing one with a dummy stuck in its mouth hardens those same eyes with the glint of judgment.

Eating

This became a major battlefield, with Small and me dug into static trenches, bombarding each other with heavy artillery.

Whilst the actual flinging of food stopped once Small reached a certain age and the battles become less messy, they were set to continue and will probably carry on until Small is big and leaves home. In the early days of solid food the stress was simply about getting Small to eat *something*. As he got older it increasingly became about getting him to eat anything that was not chocolate or potato based (maybe there shouldn't have been so much chocolate eating training early on? – see pic).

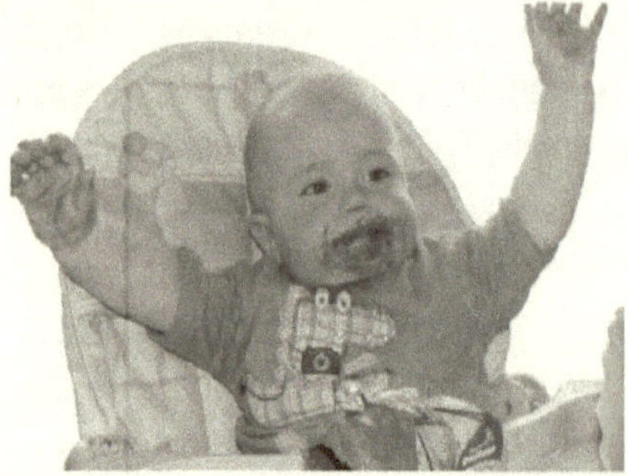

One of the most important lessons I learnt whilst raising Smalls was that Small would only do things when Small was ready to do them. This included eating. Small would only eat when he was ready. On a broad level this meant that he would not be weaned until he was ready for solid foods and on a day to day level he would only eat when he was hungry (unlike us he had not yet learnt to cram down food, regardless of hunger, simply because it was a convenient time to do so). On a slightly wider time scale it meant that one week Small would eat non-stop, the next, seemingly not at all.

This demand feeding process is natural and is actively encouraged when feeding Smalls milk. We are told that it is best for Small but sadly it is not for the parent. Actually that is not true: medically it is best for everyone to eat on demand. The trouble is, life doesn't allow demand feeding. Real life has to revolve around mealtimes. For example, it is often frowned upon to get your sandwiches out in the middle of a board meeting. Small needed to learn this, I needed to get him to eat at designated mealtimes otherwise it would always be mealtime, doubly and triply so once more Smalls popped up.

Sadly I proved to be a bad teacher for Small was rarely hungry at meal times but constantly hungry in between. Perhaps I should have stopped stuffing him with biscuits.

To return to the early food days, when it came to weaning Small onto solids, the suggested first food was a bland cereal mixed with their normal milk. The theory was that it would not be overly strange and Small could get used to the texture. It didn't work. Small didn't like the texture and it was, well, bland. I can't blame him, I certainly wouldn't eat bland cereal gloop.

We tried to give Small something tasty, like mashed banana or sweet potato. He pulled the most extraordinary faces at first but that didn't mean he didn't like it, it was just not what he was used to. At an older age we took Small 1 to a pizza restaurant to meet my wife's work colleagues. It was his first experience of pizza. From the look on his face when he took his first bite I thought that the restaurant was about to ring with screams as he tried to vocalise how disgusting this flat sloppy thing was. The contorted face and gurning continued until the pizza had been utterly consumed. It was only then that the wailing began and it only stopped once another pizza appeared.

There was a lot of advice about making your own food for Small. This had merit because we knew what was in it and it was cheaper than buying jars of pre-made gloop. The down side was that we ended up spending a considerable amount of time (in comparison to the time actual available) lovingly preparing food that was wholly rejected. For despite his early interest in new flavours Small soon decided he didn't want this solid food stuff.

Whilst we continued to try and find home-made gloop that he would eat, we ended up resorting to bought jars. In the end he discovered one variety that he liked and then refused everything else. What the heck: it contained all the nutrition he needed. I did get a slight feeling of being judged at the checkout though, when my weekly shop consisted solely of a crate of small jars of lamb hot pot, powdered baby milk, disposable nappies, nappy bags, paracetamol and wine.

A final word of observation to anyone contemplating multiple Smalls: don't expect to find a meal (any meal) that everyone in the family likes. Every meal will disappoint someone. You cannot win. I found the trick was not to set it up as a challenge in the first place, then I couldn't lose. It was the same result but mentally easier to handle.

Efficiency

Efficiency was the key to successfully managing to look after Small and the house and the garden and the doidens whilst still squeezing out some time to be with my partner and at least touching upon my own personal interests.

Ironically, in the first few days of Small's arrival there was not enough time to spend on thinking of ways to save time. My time was fully occupied making sure Small didn't die and looked reasonably presentable to the outside world; and trying to cope with sleep deprivation. Fortunately this phase soon passed and tiny, gleaming nuggets of time began to present themselves. To achieve anything beyond survival, these nuggets of time had to be mined and smelted in the most efficient way possible. For instance, when Small woke us at 23:00 (TV viewing no longer contained sex or violence because we were asleep before the watershed) I would gather together a wash and then put it in the washing machine when we were woken again at 03:00. It was hung out to dry when we were up again at 06:00.

When it comes to finding efficiencies it helps to be a basically lazy person, that way you are always looking for ways to make things as easy as possible. I begrudge spending more time on a task than it needs and will always be looking for ways to make it quicker. I am not unusual in this. Anyplace there is a paved path meandering through grass there will be an unofficial path were the grass has been worn away by all the people taking the shortest route. I tried to apply the same thinking to tasks.

A simple example of efficiency in operation that we have probably all used is cleaning a burnt pan. Rather than sticking it in the sink and starting to scrub, stick it in the sink and go and complete another task. Once it has had a chance to soak the scrubbing is easier and, overall, less time will have been used.

Personally I found great efficiency in using motion to my advantage. Looking after Small I spent a lot of time roaming around the house so I tried to make each trip as worthwhile as possible. I never moved from room to room empty handed if there was something that needed to be moved back to its proper place (and there was always something). Equally, I didn't go out of my way to move something beyond where I was originally heading. For instance, I positioned things that had to go upstairs at the bottom of the stairs (and vice versa) so that the next time I ascended I could grab an armful and get it closer to its home. Whilst you have a Small you are not going to live in a clutter free house. There will be piles of stuff everywhere but at least this way they will all be moving in the right direction and some items may even make it back to where they belong.

Conversely, I tried to keep the number of trips around the house to a minimum. If I could avoid going from one end of the house to the other to get a tool, I did. For example, I created a nappy changing area both upstairs and downstairs and kept each fully stocked with the required junk. That way I saved numerous trips up and down the stairs. Similarly, I stored cleaning products in both of our bathrooms to save traipsing to a central store.

That also leads onto another thing I found saved time: cleaning little and often. If I wiped around the bathroom every day it took no time at all, especially because the tools were to hand. If I left it to once a week it became a big chore. The same with the kitchen. If I tidied up as I went, putting things away after I had used them and wiping the top down, the kitchen was always clean and clear. If I didn't it ended up looking like a warzone by the end of the day and would take an age to tidy. It was also highly inefficient if it was untidy because I couldn't find anything and there was no space to work in, causing frustration and eating up more time.

Fads/Fixations

This was not an issue with Very Smalls. It took them a while to be aware enough of the world around them to become hooked by something. But it did happen at a surprisingly young age.

Before Small was able to say anything other than 'doiden' he became fixated by Thomas the Tank Engine. Small was throwing bricks around the living room one day with the television on in the background, mainly for me to hear adult voices to stop me going crazy. Thomas the Tank Engine came on and Small stopped throwing bricks and became transfixed. Five minutes of silence was followed by a complete meltdown when it finished.

In these days of rewindable TV I could have spent the day looping the programme again and again but those were the days of video recorders (younger readers may need to visit their local museum to see one of these devices). So, I loaded an inconsolable Small into his buggy and headed for the shops. He only calmed down once I had found a Thomas video, in the third charity shop I tried, and he could see his new hero on the cover. He then spent the rest of the day watching the video over and over. It wasn't great parenting but he *was* quiet.

The Thomas fixation lasted for 5 years and then switched off literally overnight. One day it was train track all over the lounge, the next, none. However, during the fixation years an enormous collection of wooden, metal and plastic Thomas and Friends trains and tracks was accumulated. The weight of it still presses on my shoulders as it looms in the loft above, waiting for me to find time to rehome it. The accrued cost makes me shudder. Luckily most of it was bought by grandparents.

That was not the last fad but it was the longest. As Small got older the fads seemed to fade faster, probably as he became aware of a wider range of things and more susceptible to peer pressure. Some came and went in weeks, others came and went and then return again.

A chronology of fads for our Smalls was:

- Thomas the Tank Engine
- Bob the Builder
- Club Penguin
- Ben 10
- Bin Weevils
- Puffles
- Star Wars
- Minecraft
- Marvels Super Heroes

Some of these overlapped, which was a burden because the thing about fads is, you have to have everything! And you have to have it now!! And once you have it all you go off it overnight and move on to the next awesome thing.

Small also suffered from food fads but these could be fleeting. If I was lucky he would have gone off his 'favourite thing ever' by the time he was halfway through his first plateful. Otherwise it would be a week later that he decided he didn't like it (and never had), just after I had bought in a job lot, jubilant that I had finally found something he would eat.

Fixing Things

A decision needs to be made about whether things are going to be fixed or not, preferably before anything actually gets broken.

I made the mistake of fixing one of Small's broken toys and thereafter he always expected me to be able to fix anything. If something proved to be completely unfixable (at least by me) then I had failed Small utterly.

Perhaps it would have been better to have never fixed anything. But that would have meant buying replacements, which would have been expensive.

Food Shopping

I found the best way to get through this chore was to treat it like a computer game.

In the game I had to fill my shopping cart with items from a variable list and get through the checkout without blowing the shop up.

Why blowing the shop up? Well, in my cart was a ticking bomb known as Small. I only had so long before it exploded. I had to push fast, load quickly and not deliberate over brands. I learnt product placement and developed an optimum route. I cursed loudly every time the store 'levelled up' by moving everything around, just to make the game harder.

A few games in I discovered a hidden time bonus in the baby aisle in the form of organic corn puff snacks that, if opened and feed to the Small-bomb, delayed the explosion. My game strategy became to plan this in for a third of the way around my route but I soon discovered that each time I played the game the amount of time I had before needing to pick up the time bonus reduced as the Small-bomb learnt to associate the shop with the bonus. Before long it became the first place I had to visit, even though it was at the wrong end of the store.

Once all the corn snacks have been consumed, time was up. The end of the game was indicated by the Small-bomb exploding, loudly. As I progressed up levels the time to complete the mission became shorter due to the Small-bomb's increasing ability to demolish corn snacks.

Sometimes I had to continue with an extra life in the form of additional corn snacks although later I discovered an unofficial cheat plugin to download, which upgraded the corn snack time bonus to a toffee time bonus.

There were occasions when I failed in my mission but that didn't matter because in my rush I had normally forgotten half of the things I needed and had to play the game again the next day anyway.

Garden

Pre-Small we had spent considerable time and effort on our small garden making it the perfect environment (for us). Outside the back door was a paved patio with a small waterfall tumbling down over a fake pebble river bed into a pool. Stone steps led up to the main part of the garden which was mostly gravelled to reduce maintenance (because we had so little time to spare – hah!). The beds, heavily mulched with bark, were filled with all sorts of exotic plants, kept lush by our automatic watering system.

When Small reached the toddling stage our eyes were opened and we saw our perfect garden for what it was: a Small death trap. It was a nightmare battle zone covered with hard surfaces to crash onto, gravel to choke on and steps to tumble down. It had a pool to drown in, the plants turned out to be mostly poisonous and the watering system was essentially a host of spikes sticking out of the ground.

A radical rethink was in order. The water had to go. The pool was filled in and the tumbling stream dug up and converted into a sloping path up to the garden. The stone steps were removed and replaced with a wavy slide, built into the ground at a shallow angle. This provided a much more entertaining route from the higher level of the garden down to the patio. Once Small got used to it he enjoyed it too. The only problem was the hard patio at the bottom.

We investigated playground rubber matting but it was enormously expensive. Fortunately I remembered cow mats from my days working in a plant nursery. These are large black mats that cows stand on when they are being milked because it is much more comfortable for their hooves than hard concrete. The propagation team used them in the nursery, not because they were being milked, but because otherwise they would be stood on hard concrete all day. And no, they didn't have hooves. The point is, the mats are softer than concrete and a fraction of the cost of playground rubber matting.

The spiky and toxic plants were removed and replaced with annuals to fill the gaps. Which, incidentally, attracted a lot of stinging insects.

Holidays

Holidays did not really exist for me as a house husband. The day to day grind had to continue, it just had a different background. The background was unfamiliar meaning each job took longer and was more fraught. But at least I had someone to share the burden with during what would have been normal working hours. Which meant it was not much of a holiday for my wife either.

Still, a change is as good as a rest.

Bollocks. I was glad to get back to the routines I had painstakingly carved out of the day.

Housework

This was the easy part. As much as possible I let the technology take the strain. It was all about logistics – grabbing those five minutes when I had them. I would chuck the washing in the machine first thing so I could hang the clothes out (or hurl them in the dryer – one of our best purchases ever) before I went out on my errands. That meant they would be dry when I got home ready to be folded and put away. I did not iron them, life is too short and I had a Small.

I tidied as I went, never moving from one area of the house to another empty handed if there was something that needed to be moved and put back in its place. Although I had to resist the temptation to tidy up Small's play things until Small was not there. That would have been wasted effort and potentially dangerous. At best Small would get everything back out and at worst he would have a complete meltdown until *I* got everything back out. A caveat to this rule was that I had to get rid of 90% of the play things just before mum got home from work, otherwise it would have looked like I had done nothing all day (for full details see <u>Quarter to Six</u>). The best way to do this without fuss was to bribe Small with biscuits, which distracted him long enough for the things to go away and mum to arrive. If he then got everything back out again it didn't matter.

Ignore other Parents

This is possibly the single most important thing I learnt. I don't mean I shunned them in the street. I don't even mean that I didn't listen to what they had to say, they were going through the same experience as me and may have had some good tips. But I did listen to them with a 'bragging parent' filter in place.

Humans are competitive by nature. Not necessarily outwardly, but inside we are always measuring how well we are doing by comparing ourselves to others. We cannot help it, even if the results show we are not doing very well at all.

Wrapped up in the isolated cocoon of exhaustion and stress created by living with Small there were few clues from the outside world as to how well I was doing. Therefore, when they came along they had a big impact and what other parents said about their Smalls left me feeling that I was not coping as well as everyone else. They seemed to be dealing with everything much better than me and their Smalls were all progressing so much more rapidly. What was I doing wrong?

As it happens, nothing. It seems that what people say, and believe, and what really happens can be poles apart. Neither they, nor their Smalls, were doing any better than me. Here is a list of some of the comments that left my wife and I feeling like inadequate failures and the reality of the situation:

- "Jimmy sleeps through the night and has done so since he was 1 month old." Later it was discovered that 'the night' meant 11:00pm to 2:00am.

- "Sarah loves her food; you should see her with her cheese on toast." I did, she picked at the cheese and wore the rest on her head before throwing it on the floor.

- "Mary can walk!" Mary could twitch her legs back and forth whilst being held upright, an inch from the floor.

- "Harry is almost toilet trained now." Harry cried and screamed on the potty for five minutes, producing nothing, and then wet his pants ten minutes later.

- "Owen interacts well with other children." Owen kicked and bit then wailed when he didn't get the toy he wanted.

Jumpers and Jackets

I soon learnt that life is too short to get into a battle of wills over whether or not a jumper or a jacket (or a woolly hat or gloves or a scarf) are worn or not. Small definitely reacted differently to cold than me. If he was not cold then he was not cold. But I did have to carry everything with me for when he decide that, actually, he was cold after all. I tried not to moan about this and treated it as part of my job.

As a caveat, I did insist that a sun hat was worn (when it was sunny). And sun cream (ditto).

Kit

Where to start? There were so many things we needed. Equally, there were so many things we were told we needed (mainly by the manufacturers of those products) that we really did not.

Here is a list provided by a well-known UK purveyor of baby paraphernalia that I have adapted according to my own experience (and also taking out some blatant product placement):

clothes (for first 2-3 months)

recommended

- 6-8 sleep suits
- 6-8 vests
- 6-8 bodysuits
- 2 cardigans
- 4-6 pairs of socks
- 2 pairs of scratch mitts
- sun hat
- 2 x soft cotton hats

could be useful

- jacket
- 3-4 x daywear outfits

out and about

recommended

- pram/pushchair (suitable from birth) inc;
  - cosytoe
  - weathershield
  - parasol
- infant car seat
- child view mirror
- changing bag

could be useful

- baby carrier
- travel cot
- sun blinds for car

sleep time

recommended

- moses basket & stand or crib
- later - cot or cot bed
- waterproof mattress cover
- 4 fitted bottom sheets
- 4 flat sheets
- 2-3 cotton cellular blankets
- baby listening monitor
- room thermometer
- swaddling blanket

could be useful

- wardrobe
- chest of drawers
- cot mobile
- 2 sleeping bags
- blackout blind
- dimmer switch so do not blind self and Small in the middle of the night
- nursing chair

breastfeeding

recommended

- 3 nursing bras
- 2 sleep bras
- easy opening nightwear
- breast pads
- 10 posset cloths
- breast pump
- breast milk storage bags
- bottles/steriliser
- nipple cream / shields / shells

could be useful

- breastfeeding support pillow
- nursing tops

bottle feeding

recommended

- 6-12 bibs
- 4 bottles
- 4 teats
- 10 posset clothes
- Bottle steriliser
- formula milk
- bottle brush
- compartmented milk powder storage container

could be useful

- breast pump
- breast milk storage bags
- bottle warmer

weaning (6 months)

recommended

- highchair
- larger bibs
- bowls
- spoons
- non spill cups
- teething rings

could be useful

- storage pots
- splash mat (if feeding over carpet)
- food blender
- travel highchair/booster seat

bath and change time

recommended

- nappies
- nappy sacks and wipes
- nappy cream
- changing mat
- baby sponge & face cloths
- baby towels
- baby toothbrush and paste
- baby nail scissors
- baby hairbrush and comb
- baby bath
- bath thermometer

could be useful

- bath toys
- baby toiletries
- non-slip bath mat (if using actual bath)

time to play (from birth to around 6 months +)

recommended

- baby activity gym
- lightweight rattles
- soft teddies and toys
- textured baby books
- bouncing cradle
- bath toys
- pram or pushchair toys
- light and musical toys

home safety

recommended

- smoke detectors
- carbon monoxide detector
- window catch
- safety gate/s
- socket covers
- cupboard catches
- non slip bath mat
- fire guard

could be useful

- corner cushion protectors
- play pen

It is a question of taste or circumstances whether or not any given item would make your own list. On the whole, though, most products are not ones that people would find objectionable or just plain weird. Here is a list of my favourite, genuinely available, products that are just crazy but some folk obviously buy [if that is you I apologise – but really!]:

- The iPotty – a potty with a built in iPad holder so Small can play the iPad whilst pooping. Clearly designed to distract him from what he should be doing and to train him that, if he wants to play on the iPad, he better go to the potty.

- Motion detecting belt that will auto-Tweet every time Small kicks (pre-birth obviously). I just pray nobody I know sets me up as a recipient.

- The onesie mop – a onesie with duster attachments on the arms and legs, so Small can earn his keep as he crawls around.

- Nappy alarm that will detect if Small has pooped – er…nose?

- The ride on vacuum cleaner - the go to device for graduates of the onesie mop.

- Mobile phone case with easy grip handles and teething rings for Smalls. A good lead in product for the iPotty.

- Baby toupee – to make Small look like someone he isn't for photos.

Leaving Small

The first time I left Small with a stranger he wailed and moaned and cussed. Well, why wouldn't he? I would have wailed and moaned and cussed if someone had left Small with me.

Small also kicked up a fuss but I didn't despair. I tried to view it as a good thing: if he had been quite happy to be left with a stranger, what would that have said about me.

Whilst the stranger and Small were wailing and moaning and cussing it was difficult to leave. I made the mistake of going back and trying to comfort them but it only made matters worse. In the end I realised that I had to be cold and detached. I had to walk away.

I didn't walk very far. I tortured myself and waited outside, hidden from sight. What I discovered was that within a couple of minutes the fickle duo had shut up and were quite happy in each other's company. All of my anguish had been for nothing.

Thereafter, each time Small was left the wailing and moaning and cussing became less, until it disappears altogether. That is not always the case though: Small 3 continued the routine for a very long time. This is possibly because by that stage, out of necessity, I had returned to work part time and he had to be left with a minder, one day a week, from a very young age. Although it was painful to leave him it did indicate to us that having one of us at home full time, whilst we could afford it, had been the right thing to do.

Strangely, as Smalls turn into Bigs they are more likely to wail and moan and cuss if you stick around and embarrass them by being alive.

Listening

Despite wanting to retreat into the soft, cushioned and above all sound proof room I had created in my mind, I learnt that I had to listen to the noises emanating from Small. If I could work out what they meant I had a reasonable chance of making them stop. Listening to Small ultimately meant more quiet time for me. Listening was important.

The converse was not true. Small had very little interest in listening to me. I knew this because Small never did anything I asked him to. He would not respond to my commands. I felt that this was because he was being wilful; deliberately being naughty just to goad me. This feeling was much more acutely in a public arena such as a shopping mall. Worse was somewhere like a doctor's waiting room. At least in the shopping mall everyone was moving. Those judging stares were fleeting. There was no time for them to build into tutting and pointed coughing. But Small was not being wilful, he was just not interested in 99% of what I had to say. This was because it didn't correlate with what he wanted to do (see The Centre of the Universe).

Before I worked this out I thought that, perhaps, Small was being naughty. Certainly the demon on my shoulder was whispering that all the people staring at me thought he was. Worse, they also thought that it was my doing because I so obviously did not know how to raise a Small. This resulted in me digging in my heels and becoming more forceful to show him who was boss. Sadly, it turned out to be him.

The concept I initially failed to grasp was that Small was not being naughty. Naughty is a concept invented by adults and it was not within his understanding. As adults most of us have a very good understanding or what is right and what is wrong. True there are all kinds of shades of grey (fifty, apparently) where the two abut but we can see there is a divide. We do not, however, come pre-programmed with this discernment: it is learnt behaviour, drummed into us since we were Smalls ourselves, battling with our own parent, reinforced through schooling and polished by societal pressures.

If Small had no understanding of right and wrong he could not consciously have been doing wrong. He was just doing. *I* might have viewed what he was doing as wrong but he did not. Therefore he was mightily confused by my rebuff and chose to ignore it.

So, how long would it be until Small knew right from wrong? Everybody learns things that they can see a benefit from very quickly. Lessons that have onerous results are hard to learn and we regress. Small learnt where the cookie jar was swiftly and instantly mastered how to open it. Learning not to throw his bowl of food on the floor was hard because it was a fun thing to do, so why did he have to stop. Why was it wrong? From his perspective there was no downside to it because he was living in the moment and did not understand the concepts of clean or tidy. He had a lot of background things to learn before he had a framework on which to hang right or wrong.

So, at what age could I expect Small to be able to make a judgment call on good or bad? In English Criminal Law a child under the age of 10 cannot be tried for a crime. This is because he is deemed not to have sufficient understanding of right and wrong. If the laws that ultimately define right and wrong for us tell us that it can only be properly understood when we are 10 years old perhaps I shouldn't have been judging Small as naughty in such a knee jerk way. Sure, I could start him on the learning process but I shouldn't start thinking he was doing these things deliberately to annoy me or humiliate me in public. He was not. He would start that when he was 10.

Incidentally, you may feel that the UK has set the age of criminal responsibility too high. Surely everyone knows right from wrong at a much younger age. Well, the UK has the lowest age in the European Union, for instance France sets the age at 13, Italy at 14, Denmark at 15 and Spain at 16. In the US the situation is more complex with each state setting its own age for state crimes, ranging between 6 and 12, whilst the age set for federal crimes is 11.

Living on an Island

Being a house husband was not unlike living on a desert island. Looking after Small and the house was all consuming and isolating. I became more and more introspective and self-absorbed. There was little contact with the outside world other than to obtain essentials, and much of that was achieved via the nameless, faceless internet.

Each evening and at the weekends my wife paddled over from the mainland, acting as an umbilical link to the world beyond the waves. That was the thing that stopped me losing myself utterly, going crazy and talking to the coconuts.

Not that there was anything wrong with life on the island. Apart from the squawking parrot that needed constant attention, life was quiet and there was little stress, at least in the sense I defined it at work – I was not going to be sacked (although, at times, I might have welcomed it).

In fact, life on the island was pretty good and would have been perfect if it wasn't for the fact that there was a metaphorical radio on the island that kept picking up snippets of news from the world outside. Like most news feeds, it was all bad:

- All of Small's contemporaries were doing better than Small; Alan had a tooth, Amelia could say 'dada', Alex slept through the night and Amanda was eating solids.
- Andrew's parents had bought a new car.
- Amy's parents had a new bathroom and a new sofa.
- Aaron's family was going on holiday to Disney World.
- Alysha's parents were having an extension built.

[You may think it strange that all these names begin with 'A' but see <u>Naming</u>.]

'So what?' you ask. 'Why was that bad news?'

The problem was that from the earliest age we are bombarded from every angle with the message that material 'things' are what count. We have all grown up programmed to believe that things define us. If we haven't got the latest, shiniest things then we are somehow failing. Well, everybody else seemed to be able to obtain new things and we couldn't – FAIL.

The fact that Small's contemporaries were all doing better than him was a direct fail because I was in charge: I must have been doing something wrong.

What compounded this was the fact that my head added up the things other people were achieving and attributed the total to all of them. In my head *all* the other families were achieving *all* of the goals for their Small and still managing to carry on living, i.e. buying *all* of the things.

The reality was that other families were not achieving everything: each family was achieving one of the things and that was because they had prioritised it. They had probably given up something else to achieve it. In most cases it was because both parents were still working, even if at least one was on reduced hours. They had, therefore, 'given up' being with their Small full time. I chose a different path and could therefore expect different scenery on my journey.

Anyway, there was little doubt that those 'things' had been purchased on credit. That was a temptation I no longer had to worry about: I didn't have a paid job and couldn't get credit anymore.

So, I decided to smash the radio and enjoy life on the island for a while. Before I knew it I would be rescued - and soon wish I hadn't been.

Losing Small

There was nothing quite like that feeling I got when I turned around from a moment's distraction at the park and couldn't see Small. It was like the bottom of my stomach flapping open and everything tumbling out.

Trying to keep calm, I would start scanning all the play equipment, endeavouring to remember what he was wearing so I could pick him out in the crowd. Nothing!

Heart starting to hammer, my vision would dart wider, checking the entrances, trying to see if he was attempting to get out. No!

On the move now I would run frantically from play piece to play piece, checking from every angle. Still no sign of Small!

Had he been grabbed? I glared suspiciously at every adult holding the hand of a toddler and scrutinise their Small to make sure it wasn't mine. No!!

By now my mind would be starting to draft my piece to camera, begging for information that would help me find Small (knowing deep down that when the body was found everyone would think the father was the culprit).

Facing a bleak and miserable future; a tortured life of guilt and remorse, I would suddenly hear a cheerful and innocent, "Doiden"'. Tracking the sound, hope rising, I would invariably find Small wedged in a tiny crevice that he had managed to squeeze himself into following a woodlouse or similar. The relief was instant and massive and, pulling him out by his bottom, I would swear to myself that I would never be distracted again.

'Bing bing!' Ooo, text! Nobody texts me any more…

Mastication

No, don't be shocked! Just read the title again, a little slower this time. This is to do with chewing.

Small chewed just about anything, from our doidens' ears to electrical cables to rocks. Sadly the only thing he didn't want to chew was food. He either spat it back out or choked.

Naming

When it came to naming, neither my wife nor I had any strong initial thoughts so we turned to an a-z book of names for inspiration. After struggling to decide between Jones, Smith and Harris we had to accept that the telephone directory was perhaps not the best choice and went out and bought a proper name book instead.

In my opinion it is worth scanning through the whole list before making a decision but some parents seem to find this difficult. I often joked with the parents in Small 1's antenatal group that they either had short attention spans or found names that they fell in love with extremely quickly for there was an Abigail, an Amelia, an Amy, a Benjamin and (drumroll for the parents with the greatest staying power) a Conor. I couldn't help feeling some of them had wasted 25/26th of the purchase price.

Once we had decided upon a name the next big issue was whether to reveal our choice to friends and relatives. This could prove to be a testing time, especially if we were not 100% convinced ourselves. We might have faced some disparaging remarks or, possibly worse, silence or an exclamation of 'oh' or 'ah' or even 'shame'.

So we kept the name to ourselves. We were sure that once there was an actual baby to go with the name it was very unlikely we would get any disparaging remarks. Our reasoning was that names are a very subjective matter when they are being considered in the abstract but when they are linked to a living, breathing, farting, belching, sleep deprivation inducing bundle of joy they invariably elicit a positive response. The 'oh's and 'ah's change tone and are expanded upon to 'oh, that's nice' or 'ah, what a lovely name'.

And that was how it was. Mostly. There are always those who like to say what they think without engaging any social filters so we still met the occasional, "Really?" and the odd, slightly more guarded "That's unusual." We just had to hope that they were referring to the name and not our precious, beautiful and above all, perfect, Small. We ignored any unsavoury remarks and consoled ourselves that Smalls tend to grow into their names. It is very rare to meet somebody that doesn't seem to suit their name.

If the worst case scenario should arise, i.e. Small decides he doesn't like his name, he can always change it later in life. I once had a friend who disliked his name so much that he changed it to the first three things he saw when he opened his toolbox. He was thereafter legally known as Monkey-Wrench Spanner Hammer, which *is* unusual but does have a rather good ring to it. Luckily he didn't spot the wire strippers, an awl and a screw first. Then he would have been known as Screw Awl Strippers, which sounds more like a statement of intent than a name.

That is one of the reasons it is important to spend some time thinking about names and their potential consequences. Monkey-Wrench's parents either didn't think his original name through or were mean at heart: if you have the surname Peacock you should think a bit longer before naming your son Andrew. On the face of it everything looked fine, until his school mates start shortening it to Drew. Now if you say Drew Peacock to yourself a couple of times without pausing between names you'll understand why it was a problem. Kids are crueller than adults and picked it up instantly.

A final word of caution, name books seem to come with two section; boys and girls. Pick one from the right section otherwise Mary might feel a tad aggrieved when he gets to school.

Nappies

Perhaps the first thing that jumps to mind when a non-parent hears the word 'baby' is nappies. The thought is off putting: changing nappies is repugnant. Who would want to deal with the waste products of another being? It is bad enough dealing with your own.

The simple answer is, nobody. Given the option, nobody would want to change a nappy. Thankfully, people do it though. Someone even changed mine.

Changing Small's nappies was not as bad as I had anticipated (most of the time). In fact, in the early days, when there was only milk being ingested, the waste products were particularly inoffensive, which gave me a long break-in period to get used to the process before anything really bad turned up.

Within a few weeks I was able to strip down my Small, clean it and re-dress it, in the dark, in less than a minute, whilst still 95% asleep. I lived by a military mantra: Look after you Small soldier! Your Small is your best friend. You will eat with it, walk with it, work with it, sleep with it and crap with it!

So, by the time Small was weaned I was well honed in the skill of nappy changing and was able to effect a nappy change, even in hostile territory, in a very short span of time. This was good because with solids came aroma and consistency. The more varied the input of solids, the more varied the aromas and consistency. Fortunately the nappy open phase only lasted a minute and I could deal with it; even if it might have been several times a day. It was not that bad. Strangely though, the thought of changing another Small's nappy is still as distasteful as ever.

In the early days, cleaning was with water and cotton wool. Once Small's skin had toughened up a bit I was grateful to move onto baby wipes. These are one of the best inventions EVER. Man's landing on the moon is of little significance in terms of human achievement compared to the creation of baby wipes. No parent should be without baby wipes at any time whilst is charge of a Small.

Most nappy related clean-up operations could be accomplished with two baby wipes. First the unsoiled part of the nappy itself was utilised to remove the vast bulk of any solid matter adhering to Small's skin. Next the first baby wipe was used to remove the residue solids, taking care to delve deep into any folds of skin where secreted matter could gather and fester. Then the second baby wipe made sure all skin was spotlessly clean.

If any poo remained on the skin it led to nappy rash, which made the next poo and change painful for Small and dramatically noisy for me. Incidentally, the best nappy rash treatment I discovered in the UK was Metanium, which is available in the US through Amazon.

Sometimes Small would produce a three baby wipe deposit and occasionally four were required. These episodes often involved slight leakage from the nappy which meant a change of vest and, if the leakage was extensive, a change of trousers or baby suit.

Rarely, I was treated to a cataclysmic, Krakatoa style explosion of poo from Small. Nappies were unable to contain these seismic events and a tsunami of slurry would surge up Smalls back, sometimes reaching as far as his shoulders. Some eruptions measured up to eight on the baby wipe scale. In extreme cases baby wipes had to be abandoned and Small was stripped down and held under the shower. This is one reason I always had a spare set of clothes when we were out and about.

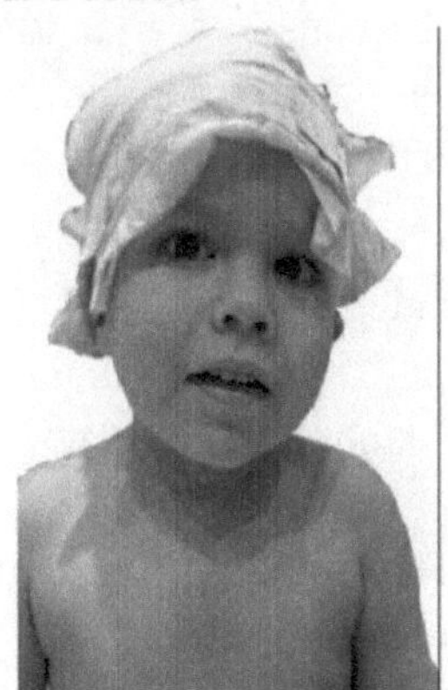

We got through a lot of nappies. My supermarket trolley was always half full of nappies and baby wipes. The other half was full of formula milk, ready meals, wine and pain killers. And once Small had mastered product recognition, toys.

When I stopped to analyse the actual number of nappies consumed by

Small it was quite frightening. I would estimate that Small got through an average of 5 nappies a day (many more than that when Very Small). Small was in nappies for at about 2½ years so that is 5 x 365 x 2½ = 4,562.5 nappies.

We had 3 Smalls so that was a total of about 13,500 nappies.

Now, if it took me an average of 5 minutes to change Small, including the time to get to the changing area and return to where I was before the incident, that meant I spent a total of 67,500 minutes or 1,125 hours changing nappies.

Put another way, if an average working day is 9 hours then I spent 125 working days or 25 working weeks changing nappies. 25 WORKING WEEKS SPENT CHANGING NAPPIES!! With holidays that is half a working year on a constant conveyor belt of nappy changing.

Even if I reduce the average change time down to 3 minutes it is still 15 working weeks – nearly 4 months doing nothing but changing nappies.

Similar sums can be done for feeding and rocking and playing and swimming and washing and cooking and cleaning and tidying the garden and shopping and… Now I know why I always felt so tired and never had any time to myself or to spend solely with my wife.

Looking at cost can be equally scary. Prices vary but at the time our Smalls were in nappies they cost about 20p each, which doesn't sound too bad. Multiplied by 13,500 though, it means we spent £2,700 on nappies.

It reminds me of the SpongeBob episode were Patrick and SpongeBob find a lost infant clam and look after him. Patrick goes out to work and SpongeBob plays mother. After a fraught day Patrick returns and is cudgelled into changing a nappy. He reluctantly does so and then utters, "It's not that bad". SpongeBob then starts opening cupboards etc. revealing all the dirty nappies. This gets steadily more ridiculous until he opens the window to show a mountain of nappies outside.

Okay, an exaggeration for a day, but not so unrealistic over a lifetime.

Incidentally, pre-Small I had not heard of SpongeBob but once Small reached cartoon age I discovered it channel flicking. Thereafter I encouraged him to watch it because it is funny and entertaining for adults, at least the first 5 times.

Though a laudable concept we didn't even contemplate washable nappies. Heavens knows how our parents coped with no disposables and no washing machines. My mother used to borrow the neighbour's twin tub (one tub to wash and one to spin) once a week to do the whole family's washing. Nappies had to be hand washed daily.

Naughty Step

Once upon a time it was possible to beat Smalls into shape, like a blacksmith hammering away at a shapeless lump of red hot metal until it became a well-tempered blade. These days that sort of behaviour is frowned upon. So how do was I supposed to transform my red hot, molten Small into a well-tempered tool?

To jump to a different analogy, to get the donkey to move you have to use a bit of stick and a bit of carrot. The stick I decided upon was the naughty step. The concept is not new, it has been around forever. In its rawest form think of the stocks where naughty people were locked in public view so that they could be humiliated or perhaps being made to stand in the corner of the classroom at school with the dunce cap on. The naughty step technique was much more subtle than that and wasn't meant as a humiliation. It was more about providing Small with a place to go where he could think about the bad thing he had done (having first been told what the bad thing was, because Small was unlikely to think anything he had done was wrong – see Listening). The theory was that Small had time to reflect and, possibly more importantly, to calm down. It also gave me time away from him so that I could take a few deep breaths. Without the two of us shouting at each other things had some chance of resolving themselves.

Like a nuclear missile, after a few deployments the mere threat of the naughty step proved sufficient to correct bad behaviour. From an adult perspective this seemed rather strange because there was nothing wrong with the naughty step. In fact it was nice and peaceful. I found it to be a great place to go and sit if I wanted a quiet time to myself because it was the one place Small did not want to be. [Other good hiding places are the toilet and the shed.]

Another excellent technique I adopted to try and get Small to comply with my wishes was the count to five. I had to state very clearly what I would like Small to do and then say I was going to count to five and the thing had better be done. Strangely this seemed to work despite there not actually being any threat of sanction. It was probably because it was seen as a challenge and, being a competitive human being, Small couldn't help but take it up. Of course, it could only be employed once Small had learnt how to count to five and stopped working once he had learnt about cunning and guile and could see that he was being hoodwinked. After the first time I received the response, "Or what?" I knew I would have to try some other form of coercion.

Or would I? According to some of the books and magazines I read, the ideal, modern parent did not need to resort to punishments at all. Their Smalls were brought up into perfectly balanced Bigs solely on a system of encouragement and rewards for good behaviour. Personally I thought that would be all very well for rhinoceroses but I didn't have a thick enough skin to put up with all the bad behaviour in the meantime.

That said, reward charts work wonders for older Smalls but only really kick in after toilet training age. Although, up until that age the simple sticker is a great reward. It is amazing how much a Small will do for a piece of brightly coloured sticky paper. For instance, our Smalls potty trained by getting to affix a new sticker to the potty each time they successfully used it.

Out and About

Despite my best efforts to avoid the situation, sometimes I had to go out with Small. What proved crucial to any successful trip was a properly stocked baby bag. This bag contained everything that I might need to survive in the outside world with Small. So that I never forgot it I stored it right near the front door where I would have to trip over it to get out.

The bag contained certain essential items:

- Nappies – at least three.
- Changing mat – lightweight fold/rollup version.
- Change of clothes (in case of Krakatoa eruption).
- Baby wipes – lots.
- Liquid hand sanitiser.
- Rattley toy and/or fabric book.
- Calpol (liquid paracetamol/acetaminophen).
- Tissues.
- Sun cream (even in the UK).
- Finger snacks, like rice cakes, once Small was weaned.

If the trip was longer (or badly timed) I would load:

- Extra nappies
- Bottles(s), either made up or with the necessary powders or cartons.
- Food, a bowl, spoons and bibs, once Small was weaned.

There was a huge range of purpose made bags to choose from but I selected one with lots of handy pockets (one insulated to keep a bottle warm), a washable linings and a built in changing mat. Like most baby related products, it was expensive but it was an investment worth making: it made life out and about much more efficient and lasted for three Small lifetimes. Fortunately, being a house husband, the the dilemma of choosing from the bewildering number of bags available was easier for me because I wanted something blokey, which cut the range down enormously and weeded out most of the more expensive designer models.

Overdraft

The subject of cost has been briefly touched upon under other headings. The cost of keeping (perhaps the wrong word – it implies a choice) a Small is high. Frighteningly high. In fact a report at the time of typing estimated the cost of raising a child to the age of 21 in the UK at roughly £230,000.

This is worrying. I have three Smalls so, according to those estimates, I will need to spend £690,000 on them. Based on current household income figures we are not going to have enough to raise them, let alone pay for everything else, like the house and the cars and the dogs and the cat and the guinea pigs and the rabbits. Or to feed and clothe ourselves come to that.

I can only hope that either the figures are a gross exaggeration, using every possible maximum for each category, or we benefit from a sudden windfall. If not then it is back to Victorian principles: we will have to sell off the least favoured Small as a chimney sweep. The cat can go too, there's a taker and not a giver if ever I saw one.

Personal Interests

Prior to having Smalls I frequently came across articles or television reports stating that 'normal' life can continue after having a Small. The gist of each was that with careful planning and time management you can have it all.

My personal experience shows that to be bollocks. You cannot have it all. Something will have to give, somewhere.

Closer analysis of the aforesaid articles shows that they were all about very highly paid business people and celebrities. Once you dug into the reports and read between the lines they were people that had sufficient funds to pay for a lot of support. Many had full time nannies and basically came home from their 12 hour shift to say good night to Small before they set off in pursuit of their personal interest. Others had varying degrees of similar support. Most had cleaners and gardeners to look after the household tasks. So, for them, the thing that had to give was money.

Our reality was that we couldn't afford to pay for support. Our household income had gone down and the household expenditure had gone up. If we couldn't afford a cleaner before Small, we certainly couldn't now. So, if we couldn't pay for the extra work to be done by somebody else then we would have to do it ourselves, which meant there was much less time for us.

Were personal interests out the window then? Not necessarily. The trick was for my wife and I to provide each other with some time to pursue our own interests. We did not have anything like the time we used to but we did get some. It was important. An hour off did a world of good. Liken it to a computer that had been left switched on for too long: sluggish, non-responsive, lagging and generally irritating. Shutting it down for half an hour gives it time to cool down and clear its temporary memory so that when it is switched back on it is ready for action again (for a little while).

Is it possible to pursue personal interests without a partner around to look after Small? Maybe. I still have a clear image of my first day in the new job as house husband. Small was 3 months old, so past the really intensive care stage, and I thought I could use some careful planning and time management to get 110% out of my day by pursuing my personal interests. My passion is road cycling. Now, I knew I obviously couldn't go out on my bike and leave Small behind, as tempting as it was. No. Bad daddy. But I could set up my indoor trainer and cycle in the house. Clever daddy.

Making sure Small was clean, fed and unlikely to explode, I dragged the dining table and chairs across the floor and pushed them against the wall, making just enough room to squeeze in the static trainer and my bike.

I chucked a play mat (one of those mats with things dangling down to provide visual stimuli and interaction, if Small is coordinated enough to reach out and touch stuff) on the floor at the far end of the table and placed Small on it. Ensuring he was comfortable and not in imminent danger of being sat on by a doiden, I scurried to the garden shed and grabbed the indoor trainer. Returning to the house I set it up.

Checking Small was still in a state of joy, or at least indifference, I returned to the shed for my bike, which I manhandled across the garden and in through the patio doors. It was a struggle to fit the bike to the trainer in the confined space but eventually the job was done.

Making sure Small was still safe and happy I sprinted upstairs to change into some shorts and get my cycling shoes. On my return Small was still staring at the dangly things so I mounted to bike and started pedalling.

Within a minute Small decided he'd had enough of staring at dangly things and started to bawl. I unclipped from my pedals, dismounted and squeezed between the bike and the table to get to Small. I rattled the gym supports turning the dangly things into jiggling things. Instant silence.

By the time I had manoeuvred my way back to the bike, re-mounted and clipped back in, Small started up again, so I reversed the process. Digging through a kitchen drawer I found a length of string. Tying one end to the support holding up the dangly things I took the other end with me back to the bike. Clipping in, I hit those pedals hard, not knowing how long I would get. All the while I spasmodically jerked on the string, making the dangly thing jiggly.

The jiggly things kept Small entertained almost long enough for me to build up a sweat. In my state of sleep deprivation and lack of exercise for three months, about three minutes. No amount of jiggling would keep Small quiet for long so I was force to call a halt to personal interests.

The next treasured golden nugget of time, when Small was quiet and happy to be alone, was spent putting the bike and the trainer back in the shed and hauling the dining table back into position before mum returned from her money earning duties.

It was a lot of effort for three minutes of riding. I don't enjoy riding on the trainer anyway. Needless to say, it never happened again.

Posset Cloths

Posset cloths are muslin squares (bits of fabric, not non-trendy followers of Islam), also known as burp cloths. They formed an essential part of my Small kit.

Posset cloths formed an invaluable barrier between Small and me after a feed. Before placing Small over my shoulder to see if he wanted to bring up any wind, I would drape a posset cloth over the area first. This was because in Small's early days he would often burp up milk after a feed, known as a posset (hence both names).

In addition to protecting my clothes, posset cloth were also used for:

- wiping Small's mouth and chin clean after a feed/possett,
- containing urine fountains when changing nappies, mopping up spills,
- sponging my brow when things were getting too hot and frantic (but not directly after the above),
- wiping my face when I wasn't quick enough to contain a urine fountain, and
- crying into.

In the same way that a chef has a tea towel draped over his shoulder or tucked into his apron, I found myself walking around the house with a posset cloth. It was not been unknown for me to visit the shops with a cloth still over my shoulder, ready for action.

Pre-natal Classes

Pre-natal classes provided us with all the knowledge we needed to get us to and through the birth process. In fact they provide far too much knowledge.

For instance, it is always a possibility that delivery may not go entirely to plan but did we really need an in-depth description of *everything* that could go wrong? True, forewarned is forearmed but not if it is going to give you nightmares. We knew there was considerable pain involved but did we actually need to watch a film of someone suffering it? Did we have to know that Small may rip apart his mother's most sensitive parts requiring stitching after the delivery? Would it not have been better to have just dealt with those things *if* they occurred? I am sure that used to be the case. Now the legal profession seems to be set on suing the medical profession for not warning people when they suffer from a complication, even though they are commonplace.

In some respects this made pre-natal classes akin to torture. A professional torturer does not just arrive with a red hot iron and start poking about with it. Nor does he waltz in with a pair of bolt croppers and just snip his victim's toe off. These are the actions of an amateur. A professional will take his time. He will show his victim some of his tools, close up, so they can see the bits of gore still mashed into the mechanisms. He will describe exactly what each tool does and then, if he is really good, he will leave his victim for a while to think about things. By the time he returns their mind will have conjured up a lot of unpleasant images and they will already be in a near broken state.

In the next session the torturer will move on to some of the more grisly tools at his disposal. The victim's mind is now running very fast and can grasp exactly what they can do even before the torturer tells them. Again, he will be left to dwell.

And so on and so forth. By the time the torturer gets to the actual physical stuff the victim has already cracked.

Similarly, pre-natal classes and giving birth.

One of the benefits of pre-natal classes was the concept that we had time to plan for the birth. In fact, we were encouraged to have a written birth plan, setting out all kinds of details such as who going to partner the mother, how the mother would like the delivery to be made, what music the mother would like playing in the background and what sorts of pain relief she would prefer.

This must surely have been an exercise to occupy the mind and take it off of the torturer's tools. Despite being an induced birth (and therefore booked) there was no room on the maternity ward at our hospital when Small 1 arrived. Being two floors away from the maternity ward, no pain relief, preferred or otherwise, was available. We were only wheeled into the delivery room five minutes before the birth so there was no question of music of any type (not that anyone would have been listening, it wasn't exactly a cosy relaxed atmosphere). And in terms of who should be present – the room suddenly filled with gowned folk, bustling about in a very calm and assured (but nevertheless underlying anxious) way, when Small refused to come into the world and a Ventouse was needed to suck him out of his refuge.

It turned out it was a very busy night/morning at the local hospital. Three out of the five babies from our ante-natal classes were born within 2 hours of each other, despite being due over a 4 week spread. There were also twins from just down the road, which meant that when Small reached primary school there were 5 kids with the same birthday out of an unusually small class size of 15. There must have been some stars lined up or some such that night. Or something leaked into the local water supply.

Primary Carer

This just sounds so much better than househusband!

In fact you can big the role up as much as you like. Here is an extract from my CV:

Primary Carer

Wood Family Child Development Enterprises

> **Role:** To nurture, develop and manage steady growth of the organisation's three primary assets in as cost effective and efficient a manner as possible. Requires methodical planning to ensure resources are optimised in addition to an ability to create crisis management and dispute resolution strategies on the fly to firefight flare ups.

Dimensions: Turnover: far too much.

Achievements:

- No loss of or major damage to the primary assets
- Developed assets to point of self-sufficiency for periods of up to 30 minutes
- Collateral assets still standing, most fixed assets still functioning and liquid assets not completely dried up
- Staff: I wish

Projects

In order to maintain my sanity I filled my life with projects. Projects gave my life a meaning beyond looking after Small and the house. They were something with a defined goal that I could aim at. They were a way of dragging some feeling of achievement back into my life; some way of proving to myself that I was still capable of doing something. Providing the project went well.

Projects included:

- Decorating.
- Gardening.
- Making things.
- Writing.

During my internship (internment?) every room in the house has been decorated at least once. The garage has been converted into an office and a utility room. The garden has been completely remodelled. Beds have been constructed, one in the shape of a train and another as a caterpillar and I have written this book, some cycling books and some children's novels. Thus I try to maintain my self-confidence and my sanity (although, after reading this book, you may feel the latter is a forlorn hope rather than a reality).

Pushchair

I used to think that buying a new car was a difficult process, fraught with all kinds of buying criteria and price related compromises. Then I discovered the world of the baby conveyance device.

Isn't a pushchair was just something on wheels to push your Small around in? Well, it is. But only in so much as a car is a metal box with four wheels that moves you from A to B.

The car analogy is probably not the best one because I knew a little bit about cars and had formed opinions about what features were important to me. If someone had asked me to imagine my ideal car it would have sprung to mind with little thought. But I had no idea where to start with a Small buggy.

My first visit to the baby hypermarket left me stunned, firstly by the vast array of buggies available and secondly by the price tags. I am not even going to attempt to cover the options here, I do not have the space. Needless to say, a visit to the store and a couple of hours chatting to a sales assistant will start to make things clearer. What I will point out is that a quick search on a popular online store in the UK revealed buggies ranging in price from under £100 to over £1,000. If money is no restriction Silver Cross had a couple of limited edition models:

- Silver Cross Aston Martin Surf 2, £3000 [I don't think you can actually surf with it].
- Silver Cross Balmoral, £5000.

Like top end cars, the only real reason to own one of these is to show that you can. It is purely a status symbol to indicate to everyone else that you have it, whilst they do not. Of course, it is a little perverse because it is highly unlikely that someone who can afford one of these models is ever going to push it, that will be the job of the nanny. It is a bit like having a Rolls Royce that is only ever driven by the chauffeur.

Nevertheless, like cars, you can pitch in and buy the most brag worthy buggy within your price range and strut about parading it like a young peacock. After struggling about the town with a juggernaut of a tandem buggy for a year (see <u>Calming</u>) I persuaded my partner that we needed a more manageable twin buggy. Yes, with its 5 point safety harnesses, lie flat seat positioning, lockable front swivel wheel (with suspension), foot operated parking brakes, ergonomic soft foam handles, removable bumper bar, sponge clean seat covers, adjustable hood and massive under seat storage it was practical (I even went and measured the width of the narrowest point of the pavement on my regular route into town to prove it would fit) but the main, unvoiced, buying criteria was that it was sporty as hell. Ferrari red, with three wheels for ultimate one handed controllability, multi-adjusting seat positioning and built in cup holders, it was the doiden's bollocks.

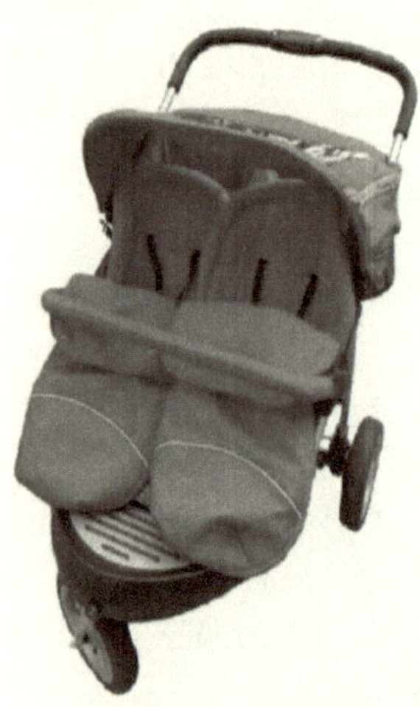

    Incidentally, remember that car I imagined at the beginning of this section? I've had to forget all about that. With a Small in tow I needed a car with a massive boot, a high ceiling for easy access and, as more Smalls arrived, pop up seats in the boot. In addition it needed roof bars and a tow bar for the roof box and trailer I needed to carry all the junk I couldn't fit in the boot. Remember that phrase about the only thing not taken was the kitchen sink? Well, we used to travel with the baby bath. Does that count?

Quarter to Six

This was the time to race around the house having a manic tidy before my wife got home. I needed to make it look like the whole house hadn't fallen apart in the last few hours.

I started with the things that would make the biggest impact for the least effort. Being able to see the floor was always a good start so I shoved all the toys back into whatever boxes and cupboards they came from, just retaining enough to keep Small occupied for a few minutes. If they were widely dispersed I swept them into a heap first. I even purchased one of those wide, industrial mop/brooms they use in large public buildings to make things quicker.

Next, I plucked all the discarded clothes from wherever they had been strewn and either put them away or at the minimum created one heap. The same went for anything else littered over the furniture. The mental impact of a clear room, apart from one large pile of junk, was much more pleasing than seeing the room with the same junk spread all over it. To the eye, clear surfaces meant neat and tidy, even if the junk was still there.

Final touches before moving onto the kitchen were to switch the television off, so that it didn't look like I had just plonked Small in front of it all day, and to spray a little polish in the air near the front door, to tease my wife's senses into thinking cleaning had taken place.

The second area of major impact was the kitchen. I cleared the worktops by scooping all the dirty cups and plates and bowls and bottles and pots and pans into the sink and/or dishwasher. If I had time, I would fill the sink with hot water and washing up liquid so that when I came back all the dirty things would be 90% clean. Starting the dishwasher up then created a background atmosphere of industry.

The reason I attacked the kitchen after the living room was because my wife would enter the living room first and then the kitchen, which meant I would get an extra minute or two to tidy as she moved through the house, saying hello to Small and the doidens on the way.

Those extra two minutes enabled me to grab some ingredients from the cupboards/fridge/freezer and place them neatly on the kitchen worktop to give the impression that I was just about to start cooking dinner. To add authenticity, I would turn on the oven and the extractor fan.

It was unrealistic to expect to do more than this in 15 minutes but if Small had gone ballistic due to lack of attention I sometimes had to squeeze in some rapid calming: I knew from experience that the impact of all of my efforts would have been lost if the first thing my wife heard on entering the house was her precious Small screaming.

Fifteen minutes of frantic panic later I could relax. I sometimes had to be rather inventive with the baked beans, tuna, rice, maple syrup, shoe polish and potato waffles I had stacked up to make dinner with though.

Reins

Personally, I am not a fan of reins for Smalls. Then again, I am not a great fan of leads for dogs either. I would rather take my dogs to somewhere they do not need a lead and can run free. Of course, if I am somewhere that my dogs cannot run free then I put them on a lead. So, perhaps, I should take the same approach to Small reins. But I don't.

The reason I don't is that I am fast and agile. There is no way a Small is going to escape from me. I can swoop like a hawk.

My dad can't though.

My parents came to visit and offered my wife and me a rare opportunity to have some time together, without Smalls, by taking them into town, to play in the park and have a look in the shops. Hooray!

We repaired to bed (so tired) but half an hour later the phone rang: Small 1 had run off and could not be found. Grandad had been left in charge and was walking to the playground, pushing Small 2 in his buggy whilst Small 1 walked alongside. Suddenly Small 1 had bolted, laughing over his shoulder expecting grandad to give chase like daddy always did. Grandad was left with Sophie's choice, did he abandon Small 2 in his buggy and chase down Small 1 or chase after Small 1, pushing the buggy but knowing he would be a lot slower than the rapidly disappearing Small 1? He hurried on as fast as he could whilst pushing the buggy but Small was incredibly fleet; he had rounded a corner and was already out of sight.

You can imagine the panic. We were in the car in moments, tearing towards town, scouring the streets for any trace of Small 1. After ten minutes of fruitless searching in the town we split our efforts. I raced back to the house on foot, following the route I normally pushed the buggy, in the hopes that Small 1 was making his way back home. Meanwhile my wife hurried to the police station to report the incident. And found Small 1 sitting behind the desk eating a bag of crisps!

Small 1, having realised that grandad was not chasing him, had started to walk home. However, when he came to a road he had stopped because he knew he should not cross roads on his own. He had sat down on the pavement and waited for grandad to catch up. Before grandad could catch up, a well-meaning elderly couple had come along and escorted Small 1 to the police station, where the nice policeman gave him a bag of crisps.

So, what had been learnt?

- By us: not to send Small 1 out with his grandparents without reins.
- By grandparents: not to offer to take Smalls out ever again.
- By Small 1: if you run away you get to meet nice people, some of whom may give you crisps.

Safe Place

There were no safe places, neither for me to hide in nor for my valuable ornaments. Once Small could move he was everywhere at ground level. Once he could climb he was everywhere. True, there were some high shelves I could squeeze ornaments onto but Small soon devised a way to knock them down. Either he constructed some form of trebuchet to hurl wooden bricks or would pull the cat's tail so that it bolted to safety on the high shelf, hurling everything to the floor in the process.

And as he grew more adventurous he discovered me skulking in the toilet and eventually even found my bolthole in the shed.

Sail with the Tide

Nothing could be done quickly or spontaneously with Small. Firstly, I had to wait until Small was ready before I could go anywhere. He had to be fed, changed and happy, with all his appropriate comforters. Then I needed to gather a multitude of things together to deal with Small whilst we were out because he would soon need feeding and changing again. There were only small windows of opportunity and if I missed one then, like the tide, I would have to wait for the next to roll in.

Sleep

I became seriously sleep deprived, especially in the first few weeks. There was no avoiding this. As a househusband it was my duty to take the brunt of the night shift because my wife had to be able to function at work in the daytime. If I fell asleep at the table no one was going to sack me (sad but true).

I have vivid memories of being up for a couple of hours at a time most nights with Small 2 who just did not want to sleep between 2:00am and 4:00am. Trying to put him down just caused a lot of noise, which meant both adults were missing sleep, so to make sure my wife could sleep I would take Small 2 downstairs and rock him whilst watching TV. At that time the only programme showing, other than commercials, was competition poker and I became quite an armchair expert, and addict. Small 2 kept up the routine until he was two.

He was unusual though. The other Smalls began to sleep for longer periods at about 4 months, once their Moro, or startle, reflex faded. This is a reflex that causes Small's limbs to jerk in response to certain triggers: a loud noise, a change in temperature, sudden movement, even a bad dream. The reflex disappears by 4 months.

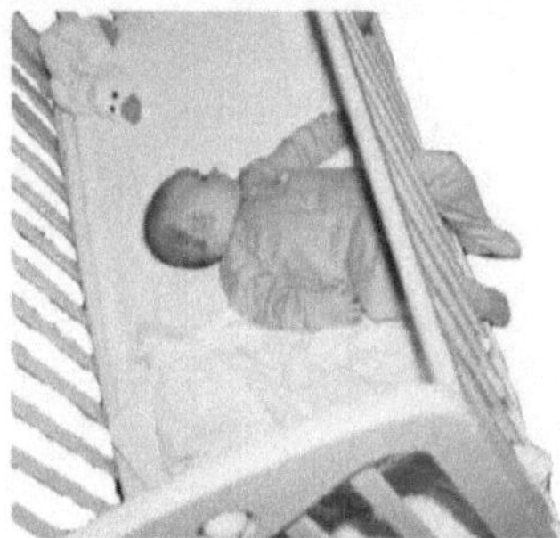

A full 8 hours sleep was not achieved much before 6 months. That's 8 hours for Small. If we went to sleep a couple of hours after Small we only got 6, which would have been ok for a day or two but not continuously.

Before long I became so exhausted I could sleep anywhere. Unfortunately I was so wound up and wired into Small that I lived in a state of perpetual alertness and would wake at the slightest mummer from him. I used to sleep so lightly that I could be up, in Small's room ready to take action, before the first cry erupted from his lungs.

Whilst this has been covered elsewhere, I tried to ignore other parents when they told me their Small had slept through the night since he was born. It made me feel inadequate. It also made me want to rip their heads off. Neither was a good emotion, although the latter had more merit. It proved not to be true anyway.

It should be pointed out that when faced with more than one Small the problems increase exponentially. Just as Small 2 has finally decided that he wants to sleep through the night, Small 1 will enter the nightmare phase, at its peak between the ages of 2 and 6.

Sleeping Aids

I have always found that the best sleeping aid is wine, white not red. Failing that anything alcoholic. Small would not drink alcohol so we had to find something else.

A good trick when Small was Very Small was to wrap him tightly in a swaddling blanket. Apparently this replicates the feeling of being in the womb and provides Small with comfort and reassurance. It seemed to work with our Smalls.

Motion was also excellent for putting Small to sleep. There are escalating stages of motion therapy:

Stage 1 - Rocking

A rocking motion was a great trigger for sending Small off to sleep. Though it seemed strange, the faster the rocking the more effective it was, at least it was with our Smalls.

In the early weeks we found a rocking crib very useful. We also invested in a rocking chair, which was great because we could sit down get some rest ourselves. Without these devices we would have had to do the work manually using the calming techniques listed under Calming.

Stage 2 - Pushchair

When rocking failed to put Small to sleep, the next stage was the pushchair. Very often a push around the block (a few times) would do the trick. Again, our Small liked to move fast. The main dilemma was, once Small was asleep, did I try to move him into his cot? He would sleep longer if the manoeuvre was a success but if he woke I faced another few laps of the neighbourhood. If it was a night sleep then there was no option, he couldn't sleep for long periods in the pushchair.

Stage 3 - Car

When stages 1 and 2 produced no results, or it was raining and cold outside and I wanted to bypass stage 2, then the next option was the car. Two of our Smalls would invariably fall asleep in the car (the third **never** slept in the car). I became unduly familiar with every twist, turn, lump and pothole in the crazed network of lanes within a 5 mile radius of our house, lanes that 95% of people in the town were not even aware existed. The car trip would always work for Smalls 1 and 2 but moving them from the car to their cot was akin to defusing a bomb. Well, not that akin, if it was I would be dead a hundred times over.

Indeed, whatever method had been used to induce Small to sleep, often the trickiest part was the transfer into the cot/crib without waking him up again. With much trial and error I developed a generally fail proof technique.

First I had to move the sleeping Small onto my shoulder, keeping a firm pressure on his back. This was particularly tricky if I had encouraged Small to sleep using the pushchair or car technique. I often had to carry out a secondary rocking session once Small was on my shoulder to re-settle him.

From cuddle on shoulder to easing Small into the cot was the next tricky stage. With firm pressure on his back, I gently leant over the cot until Small's back was as close to the mattress as I could bend. Then, sliding a hand between his chest and mine, I applied a slight pressure to his chest and eased him onto the mattress. I would then allow him to settle with one of my hands on his back (against the mattress) and the other on his chest. All this gentle pressure harkens back to the swaddling blanket, replicating the comforting pressures of the womb. Then, gently, oh so carefully, I eased the hand between Small and the mattress out, keeping the other hand in place, gently pushing Small onto the mattress. When Small had settled, I slowly, oh so slowly, eased the pressure of the push, timing each reduction in pressure with Small breathing out. Once I had no pushing pressure it was time to slowly withdraw the hand, again timing movements with breathing. Despite the feeling of euphoria when my hand was free of Small I had to refrain from doing a jig: I still had to get out of the room.

I had mapped the minefield of Small's room in my head; I knew every squeak producing floorboard and my questing toes could deftly avoid these threats (and any squeaky or rattling things dumped around) as I made a phased withdrawal to the door, being ready to return to Small at the slightest twitch to apply a hand to his chest to resettle him. Once out of the room I would gently swing the door closed. Now I could jig. But not on the squeaky floorboard outside the door.

Small Negotiation

Small was the best negotiator in the world. His secret was, he never gave in, he just kept on. And on and on and on. Non-stop. Relentlessly demanding the same thing over and over, never letting up. Constantly repeating the same thing until I couldn't stand it anymore and cracked. The reason he was able to do this was that he had no thought in his head other than the thing he wanted, nay, desperately needed. He was not constrained with thoughts of consequence or conscience. He did not have a demon sat on his shoulder nagging him that he really didn't need this hassle. Nor the one on the other shoulder whispering that constant arguing with a Small must be causing some permanent damage to the Small/parent relationship.

More than anything though, Small did not have a million other things pressing on his attention and time. He could spend as long as he liked making his case and he did. I either had to learn to deal with the million other things with the constant background noise of Small or capitulate. Although capitulate might be the wrong word because it implies surrendering on terms. That might have been possible if I had caved at an early stage but if I had hung in there until breaking point I would normally flip 180 and surrender totally, conceding to all of Small's demands utterly.

Small's Perspective

Battles with Small occurred on a daily basis. Many of them never left the confines of my head but they were still there.

I learnt that the best way to minimise, or at least quickly resolve, these battles was to try and see things from Small's perspective, to put myself in Small's shoes/booties/socks and try to imagine the incident from his point of view.

The thing I had to take on board was that Small was not a mini me. He did not have adult reasoning and experience. He had needs that were urgent, immediate even. I had received some training in this area from having a pregnant wife. He also has no concept of responsibility or accountability. He was the only thing that mattered and he had no thought for others, or even any concept of others in the early weeks.

So, based on that, was there any point raging that Small would not take his bottle or eat his food? Did I really think he was doing it just to thwart me?   If I was trapped against the cliffs with the tide rising, would I rage at the moon or just accept that it was the wrong time to be on the beach?

Stress

The stress of being a house husband was peculiar in that, from the observation platform of the person I was before I had a Small, life should have been easy. I was sat at home with just a few chores to do. I mean, how long could it take to clean the house and do a bit of shopping? Everyday should have been like the weekend.

Well, that was true. Until I factored in Small. Tidying the house would have been easy, if the untidiness was at pre-Small levels. Shopping would not have been a hassle, if I hadn't had a Small-bomb in the trolley. Producing meals would have been simple, if I wasn't doing it 5 times a day. Washing would have been no problem if it was still a load a week instead of a load a day. And I was trying to do it all with a Small in my arms and when my mind and body were wrecked by weeks of sleep deprivation.

"Ok," said the pre-Small me, "life is a bit busy but it can't be stressful because you haven't got a boss breathing down your neck all day long, demanding results. You're in charge and you call all the shots."

Ha ha ha ha! No. Small was in charge. He was the boss and there is no work boss in existence that is as demanding as Small was. There are not many real life bosses that will literally scream and scream until their demands are satisfied. And even those that do exist, will at least let you know what their demands are before they start screaming.

No, life as a house husband was not without stress.

One of the main causes of stress was trying to deal with things that were, essentially, beyond my control but for which I was deemed to have responsibility. Such was my relationship with Small. He was a force of nature but the world was looking at me to contain him. When is the last time you successfully told your boss to shut up and get a grip?

In some ways the stresses of being a househusband were less than those of working life. The financial markets were not going to crash if I couldn't get Small to eat his lunch and the world was unlikely to plunge into recession because I forgot to buy the cornflakes. But the thing about stress is that it is always there. It is a natural function that keeps us on our toes, always alert. There is no such thing as a stress free life. Life's pressures expand to fill the stress bucket available. If you remove the current stresses from your life, secondary stresses, that before were mere inconveniences, brushed away as irritants, become bigger and more frightening. They grow and mutate to fill your stress space. If you kill those off, the next level of stresses start to take over.

So, maybe the stresses were on a smaller scale but they didn't go away when I clocked off for the day because *I didn't* clock off for the day. There seemed to be no time when there was not some form of pressure on me to complete a task. It was relentless and my stress bucket was always brimming.

Swimming

Swimming was an excellent way of tiring out Small. The downside was that it was also an excellent way of tiring me out.

That is not strictly true, it was not the swimming that tired me, it was the process of getting to the water so that actual swimming could take place and then from the water back to home.

There was a bewildering paraphernalia of things that I needed to pack in order to take Small swimming. Swimming kit at school used to be a pair of trunks rolled in a towel. I still needed that, one for me, one for Small. That was fundamental: they wouldn't let us in the pool without at least the trunks. In addition I needed, depending on the age of Small at the time; a swimming nappy (failing that an ordinary nappy but they bloated up alarmingly in the water), a float seat, arm bands, a float belt, a separate float or a toggle/woggle/noodle and goggles. As Small got less Small there was the additional need for balls to play with and things that sink and can be collected from the bottom of the pool by diving. Then there was the shampoo and something to shower all the chlorine off after the swim. And the final thing I had to pack was a drink and a snack for Small after swimming. That was vital. Without it Small would explode from exercise induced hunger and any chance of getting him to sleep (the main purpose of the trip) would be lost.

I found it best to pack my bag the evening before the swimming exploit, after Small had gone down for the night (or part of the night). Thinking was clearer when Small was not in the background and I was less likely to forget things. In the morning all I had to do was remember to wedge the bag in the bottom of the buggy. Once we reached the toggle/woggle/noodle stage I had to get fairly creative with that. Oh, and I had to remember to wedge Small in the top of the buggy.

Once at the pool I faced the first major drama: getting changed. The pool changing room was a frightening place for Small. It smelt funny, was much hotter than outside and was usually noisy, with screaming kids and shouting parents battling each other behind their cubical doors. If we were lucky we would get one of the family cubicles that had a little more room and either a play pen or mat with a strap to contain Small whilst I juggled with all the paraphernalia. If not I had to use my contortionist skills to make sure

Small didn't fall from the bench whilst I juggled.

For the dry change, before the swim, I found it best to get myself changed and then change Small, aeroplane emergency style. Unless Small was already screaming, in which case I reversed the order, thinking he was probably too hot.

Once changed, the next task was to locate enough lockers, close to each other, that would take the load of all the things not going to the pool. Now, with me sporting several key armbands, we could finally make our way to the water.

My approach to water, from as young as I can remember, was to just leap in and get the shock over with. This seemed to be frowned upon when you had a Small over your shoulder. Instead I had to slowly ease into the water, either by walking from the shallows or gingerly climbing down the steps.

On our very first trip Small was not overly impressed with the pool. The water was cooler than his bath and considerably rougher thanks to all the older kids breaching the no bombing rule. Small's face crumpled and his mouth opened wide in protest. Trying to remain calm I made suitable soothing noises. When that didn't help I swished him around a bit. His face uncrumpled and broke out into a grin. Encouraged I swished faster. His face crumpled again so I slowed down until the grin returned. Soon he started to splash around and giggle gleefully.

That lasted about five minutes before he started to get cold and I found myself out of the pool and in the shower, muttering about how much effort I had gone to for a few minutes in the water. But as Small got bigger the roles reversed and I started to make, 'let's get out,' noises, long before Small was ready to leave.

Either way, once through the shower the next phase was the reverse of the changing drama. This was worse because now we were both wet and cold. Suddenly the changing room did not feel overly hot; it was a cold, slimy, miserable, dank and clammy place where I had to wrestle with various lockers whilst maintaining a grip on a wet, slippery Small. Then I had to fight for a vacant cubicle and try and squeeze everything inside, keeping our dry clothes out of the puddles on the floor and the bench.

With the wet change there was no question, Small got changed first whilst I shivered: better that I was cold than him. Anyway, by the time he was changed I had vibrated most of the moisture from my body. Once Small was dressed (he usually needed a layer more on than when he came in) I would perform a record breaking change.

When we were both dry and warm we would head to the café where Small would have his bottle, or snack and drink once he was older.

Ta dah! Swimming done and it was back in the buggy to tramp home. If I was lucky Small would doze off on the way and I would be rewarded with some Small-free time, provided I could get him indoors without waking him.

Once there were multiple Smalls, the swimming dilemmas expand exponentially: there was more paraphernalia, less space in the changing room, multiple chances of screaming with one setting the other off, more lockers were required, Small 1 would want to get out of the water and Small 2 wouldn't, Small 1 would freeze whilst I dressed Small 2 and one of them wouldn't go sleep on the way home.

Of course, swimming was not all just about getting my Smalls to sleep. I would be failing if I didn't mention the joy inherent in swimming with my Smalls (not in my smalls). Water offered them the sheer enjoyment of unrestricted limbs, expressed in freely given laughs: it was pure fun. Until it was not and they wanted to get out.

Targets

When Small first arrived I found myself in unknown territory, exploring the pitfalls and blast craters in NoMansLand. Rather than stumble around in confusion I needed to focus. I needed something to concentrate my efforts on: I needed targets.

Targets were safe. Targets were familiar. If I hit my targets I was doing all right. So, I looked around for targets.

The first target I set my sights on was weight gain (not mine, Smalls). The medical team had issued me with a book full of charts with lines and numbers. There were dates to be filled in, weights to be recorded, and lengths to be measured.

I could see that Small should weight x lbs/kgs by week y so I set off to the health clinic to have him weighed and measured. When I arrived a gaggle of mothers had beaten me to it and were already stripping down their Smalls. Waiting for a changing mat to become free I was feeling nervous but excited to see if I was getting things right.

The nerves didn't help my yet to be honed and polished Small stripping skills as I fumbled with miniature poppers and buttons but soon Small was naked and bawling in the scales. A bead of sweat trickled down my nose as I anxiously awaited the results. Small had gained 1lb. First I breathed a sigh of relief that things must have been going right. Then, "Yes! In your face!! (In whose face was not important.) My Small's the best. Na na na nah na!" All of this was of course in my head. With an air of calm I asked modestly, "Oh, that's quite good isn't it? Well done Small."

Fumbling Small back into his clothes I basked in the reflected glory. The sad reality was, nobody else cared: they were all wrapped up in the closeted worlds of their own perfect Smalls.

It all became a bit obsessive [can you be a bit obsessive?]. I manically scurried back and forth from the clinic getting my fix on weights, mostly for the reassurance that I was plotting the right course in the wilderness of parenthood, but partly for the sense of achievement. It was a sad little isolated world I was living in right then.

Later there were other goals and targets to fret needlessly about:

- 1st tooth
- 2nd tooth
- 3rd tooth etc
- 1st word
- 1st solid food
- Turning over
- Sitting up
- Crawling
- First bruise
- First item posted in the dvd player
- Standing
- Falling
- First blood leakage
- 1st step
- Toilet training

I had read about when these things should happen. When they happened ahead of schedule there was quiet jubilation in the camp. If all the other Smalls reached the target first I would fret and worry. What had I done wrong?!

Nothing. I later learnt that Small will do all of these things in his own time. There was no point driving myself into a frenzy about it. Been there. Done that. I didn't get, or deserve, a T shirt.

Food was one of the main trials. Small didn't want to eat the amount the packet said a Small his age should. Small would shrivel and die. Small would not eat the gloop I'd lovingly cooked and then destroyed in the blender. Why did I bother? I'd eat it myself! Mmm? Well, maybe not. There was more food on Small than in Small: with his head waving to and fro in evasive manoeuvres, I plastered it on in thick layers in the hope that some of it would be ingested, either swallowed or absorbed through the skin.

Eventually I would wave the white dish cloth of defeat and clear up with one eye on the clock trying to figure out how long I had until the next scheduled battle.

Meal after meal, day after day the war continued. Other Smalls were eating. Their parents were gushing about it every time I saw them (and I couldn't avoid seeing them because they positively glowed). Maggie was eating cheese on toast and Freddie was tucking into roast dinners!

Then one day, miraculously, as I slumped defeated over the highchair, gloop drying in clumps in my hair, Small picked up his own spoon and started shovelling the gloop down like he'd done it all his life.

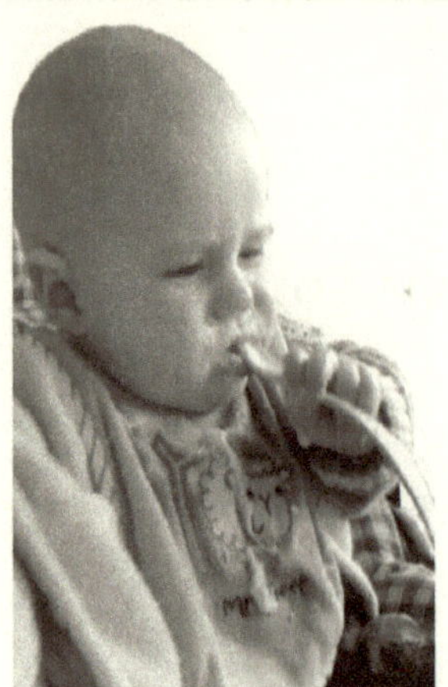

Hooray! I'd done it!

No, I hadn't. Small was just ready for it. He wasn't before.

In evidence I can proffer the fact that when Small 1 was born it was generally accepted medical wisdom that Smalls should be weaned onto solids at 3 month. When Small 2 was born (only 15 months after Small 1) it was then accepted medical wisdom that Smalls should be weaned at 6 months. We struggled to feed Small 1 solids for 3 months, until he was 6 months old. With Small 2 (and 3) we had little difficulty. So, new medical wisdom, at least as far as our Smalls were concerned, is better.

This, 'wait until they are ready' knowledge was of greatest use when it came to toilet training. We ignored the pressures created when all of Small's contemporaries seemed to be toilet trained. We reasoned that Small would not do it until he was ready and it would be even more messy and unpleasant than the food debacle if we tried to force the issue. When he was ready he went from nappies to dry pants extremely rapidly with very few accidents.

Incidentally, it turned out that the cheese on toast that Maggie was eating was really just nibbling the cheese and Freddie's roast dinner was licking gravy off the spoon.

Teeth

The first tooth erupting through the gum of Small was a time of double celebration. Not only was it a major milestone for him to reach but he had managed to get there before all of his peers, which provided me with an opportunity to gloat, modestly.

The joy turned sour once I realised that teeth needed to be cleaned. Here was another battle to have with Small. First I had to get him used to me violating his personal space and shoving an alien thing, that tasted disgusting, in his mouth. Then, once that had been mastered, I needed to try and persuade him that it would be a good idea if he did it himself.

What followed was a constant battle with daily reminders that looks set to continue until Small is big enough to leave home and take responsibility for his own teeth.

In the meantime I have to deal with the dentist.

Even the dentist waiting room is like a torture chamber with its coffee machine, inviting scolding burns to the fiddling Small, the dripping water dispenser providing a background form of Chinese water torture and the horror pictures of rotting teeth cycling around on the TV monitor.

The examination itself leaves me with all those dreadful feelings of a college exam. Have I/Small been looking after those soft delicate teeth properly? Will I/Small pull off a pass?

The first filling was a dreadful moment. FAIL!

Whilst on the subject of teeth, Small 1 managed to kill one of his front teeth not long after he started toddling: he stumbled in the garden and landed tooth first on a flower pot. There was a lot of blood because the tooth had sliced into the soft inner lip. There was also a lot of wailing and screaming and charging about, which eventually got us to the doctors, where it was declared that Small would live, so we quietened down.

Teething

I have separated out the pain or producing teeth from the pain of looking after them. For some Smalls the teething process can be quite dramatic (our Small 2), for others no issue at all (Small 1), with a whole range in between (Small 3). So, from about 3-4 months, this was another thing to add to my list of things to check if Small was unhappy.

If it was teething pain causing the current outburst from Small it was time to reach for one of two vital stock items in our medical cabinet (or both if it was severe): Calpol (Tylenol in the US), a liquid form of paracetamol (acetaminophen in the US) and Ashton & Parsons Infant Teething Powders. The latter is an old school, natural remedy, that comes in little paper folds and is poured onto the tongue. They are available in the US but an alternative is Nelsons Teetha Powder. There are also numbing gels that are rubbed into the gums.

Whilst teething, Small chewed on everything in sight. This was more likely to end up with things getting soggy than any real damage being done. It was certainly not as bad as having a puppy. One of mine chewed through an LP case and crunched up several vinyl LPs. [For younger readers, LPs were 12" discs of plastic with grooves on that stored music to be replayed using a record player. They predated CDs, which are themselves now almost redundant.] We thought it wise to invest in some teething rings though. The best ones were filled with gel and could be cooled in the fridge.

One side effect of teething is dribble. Small 2 was a champion dribbler. From the moment he started teething he had to wear a bib at all times. He saturated about 10 a day. I also took to wearing a posset cloth over my shoulder most of the time whilst at home, to prevent moist shoulder syndrome whenever I picked him up. It became such a permanent fixture that I often forgot to take it off when I ventured outside.

Television

Whilst being a house husband I ended up watching more television than I ever had before. Most parents do. Of course, most parents would deny this but it is true nonetheless.

Watching may be the wrong word but the television was always on, forming the background of my life as I trudged zombie like from task to task. In the early days it provided quasi human contact, the chance to hear another human voice. It was a link to the outside world, reminding me that, for some, life went on.

It was not long before the mindless daytime programmes morphed into mindless children's programmes and from that point onward the only adult (meaning not children's) television that could be watched was after Small had gone to bed. I had done an excellent job at training Small that the television should always be on and now he was in control it would be showing programmes he liked. I was on permanent channel changing call until I managed to train him to use the remote.

I console myself that Small has not turned into an addict. He does not spend all his free time stuck in front of the television. He's discovered YouTube on his phone now. This is much better because it leaves the television free for me! At least it would if I wasn't out ranked by Smalls 2 & 3.

The Centre of the Universe

It took me some time to realise a fundamental truth that would help me to understand Small and the way he acted: Small was the centre of the universe. Everything else in the universe was there to satisfy the needs of Small. There was no other reason for anything else to exist.

Small did not care about me. I was merely there to provide Small with the things he needed. The only importance I had was as the main provider of the things that Small needed.

Small was totally selfish. He was the epitome of selfishness, the ultimate egotist.

That may sound a tad judgmental but it is not supposed to be. It is merely realistic. To adults, being selfish is seen as a bad thing. This is because adults have had time to learn what is right and what is wrong. That is, what our parents and society as a whole have taught us is right and wrong. From that platform we can look at a selfish person and judge them. A Small has no concept of right or wrong. They have not weighed up their behaviour, seen it as bad and then decided to act that way anyway. They are, in fact, acting completely naturally, using default human behaviour. Survival means looking after number one. Thinking about others is a learnt behaviour that will develop over time. The problem for the parent is that it takes a long time to learn. Some pick the habit up early. Others never manage it completely. Most get the idea once they reach adulthood; a bit late for the parent. Incidentally, the appreciation of a good view follows a similar evolutionary timescale.

Having no concept of accepted protocols, Small displayed his selfishness loudly. When he had a need he let me know. And Small was constantly in need.

As a baby most of Small's needs were predictable: food, changing, sleep, too hot/cold, not well or just wanting entertainment. If I kept going through the list, over and over, my job was done.

Once Small started to understand his environment and had more stimuli he began to realise that he had a lot more needs than he had previously perceived. Or at least, he now needed much more specific things within the same broad categories. When he was hungry it was for a specific thing, normally something he has just seen advertised on the television. If I didn't see the advert and had to translate the need from Smallish I was in trouble. Even if, by chance, I had such a thing in the cupboard I might never have realise it. The only solution was to put Small in front of the cupboard and let him find what he wanted. He either found it or forget about it as he emptied everything onto the floor.

Thoughts and needs could flit through Small's head with alarming rapidity. For example, he may have communicated a desperate need for his favourite rice cakes. I would go to the kitchen, grab a plastic plate, dump a couple of rice cakes on it and hurry back only to find that whilst I was away new thoughts had sparkled into live, eradicating any old thoughts, and he now needed chips. What did I think I was doing bringing him rice cakes? Rice cakes were 30 seconds ago!

As a result of the inherent self-centred nature of Small and my own, learnt, self-sacrificing nature I spent a large proportion of my time dealing with the needs of Small. When Small 2 appeared (and so on), that proportion grew exponentially.

In order to deal with so many needs I had to be efficient. Each need had to be dealt with immediately and rapidly, which was fine, providing I could decipher what the need was. All too often things turned ugly because either I did not understand what Small wanted or he didn't actually *know* what he wanted, just that he needed *something*. Hopefully the thing he needed was a good shouting match, because that was invariably what he got.

Time

Before Smalls arrived on the scene I was busy. There was never enough time to get everything done. Life was a constant treadmill that never stopped with all sorts of things getting in the way of what I really wanted to be doing.

Hah! What was I thinking! Compared to life with Smalls I had nothing to do. In fact I struggle to recall what I did do. I can't fathom how I used up all the time I must have had on my hands.

Small consumed my time. He gorged himself on it. I had a lot more to do because Small was there and a lot less time to do it because Small kept distracting me from it.

Two Smalls was worse. Right up until the time they could start to entertain each other. As soon as Small 2 got to the toddling stage my Smalls started to play together. True, this usually ended in tears and recriminations but for a short while I was freed from entertaining Smalls and could get on with the washing, cleaning, vacuuming, dusting, gardening and tidying up in peace. It was amazing how much more productive I was without the constant interruptions.

Toilet Training

Shudder.

I felt very much behind when Small's contemporaries started toilet training. I tried to ignore the other parents as they bragged about how well their Smalls were doing. I knew that game and was a better player. In a race it doesn't matter who starts first, only who finishes first.

I watched the trials and tribulations, the difficulties involved, and held back, knowing that Small would have no idea what to do. Learning from the eating trial I knew there was no point trying until Small was ready and he had shown no signs that he understood base bodily functions other than that quiet smile of satisfaction when they were successfully performed.

I waited and waited, watching the others stumbling further and further ahead, until Small finally started to show the signs. What signs? Well, for him it was not being at all happy in a dirty nappy. Of course that was after the event but showed he was starting to be more aware. This was very shortly followed by him disappearing into a corner and going red in the face before filling his nappy. Now this was action before the event which indicated that he knew what was about to happen. This was the time to get the potty out. All I had to do was watch him, eagle eyed, until he made a move for the corner and then swoop in with the potty so the deed could be done in the right place. And buy a potty of course.

And so it was that Small learned very quickly and would soon go and find the potty instead of the corner when the feeling came upon him. Sticking a star on the potty after each successful use helped. Very soon the potty was plastered [with stars – we did clean it]. In fact Small was walking around accident free (virtually) whilst most of his counterparts that had started toilet training months before were still having regular 'mishaps'. They were still not really ready.

Ok, Small didn't win the race but he did win the game. It didn't matter that Small was still in nappies when his friends seemed to have left them behind. Small got there when he was ready and avoided all the accidents and the stress of failing (for both of us) along the way.

Incidentally, when it came to the potty I rid myself of it as soon as possible. I bought one of those inset seats designed to prevent Small disappearing down the U bend and moved him onto the toilet proper; that was what it was there for after all.

Public toilets and Smalls were interesting. Small 3 was [is] quite vocal and forthright. He would think nothing of declaring very loudly from the booth that he was, "Doing a massive poo now," or shouting, "I'm weeing and pooing at the same time now," before informing me that, "You can wipe my bum now". Note the imperative 'now' used in each declaration: Smalls live in the present, unlike adults who tend to dwell in the past, when they are not dreaming and hoping for the future.

As a final point, the common rule that it is polite to leave the toilet seat down and the lid closed is NOT a good one if all your Smalls are boys. In our house the rule is to leave the toilet seat up, otherwise boys wee all over it. No matter how many times they are told they still think they are accurate and will miss the seat. They are not accurate and often miss the toilet completely. Leaving the seat up is a good rule, it saves sitting in a puddle.

Toys

Families generally have much greater disposable income these days and toys are, relatively, much cheaper than they were when we were Smalls. I have to believe this, otherwise I cannot possibly account for a house that was bursting at the seams with toys. They were everywhere, in every room.

We even had a 5 foot by 7 foot shed in the garden dedicated to outdoor toys. It was full of tractors and bikes and seesaws and balls and paddling pools and lawn games and ...

We converted our garage into a utility room and an office. Whilst, out of necessity, we can beat a path to the washing machine, the computer and filing cabinet were soon buried under an overflow of toys.

The loft is still stuffed with toys that have been outgrown. The main fetish of Smalls 1 & 2 was Thomas and Friends and there are plastic tubs full of wooden and plastic track and buckets full of wooden, plastic and metal trains [builders buckets are cheap and great for storing and moving bulk loads of small items such as trains]. Small 3 was not interested in trains so we have been trying to lighten the weight from the rafters but every time we bring some down to get rid of them they suddenly become Smalls' favourite things, so they stick around in the house before they can be put back in the loft in the hope that they will be forgotten again. Then we sneak them down again, they are discovered and the cycle continues.

Every time I consider the cost of the toys it makes my eyes water, so I try not to. Then again, it is only money. What else would we do with it? Well,
...

So, how did it happen? Why are there so many toys? It was a combination of <u>Small Negotiation</u> (see separate listing) and the sheer pleasure it gave us to see them happy. And whilst Small was distracted with toys I could get on with stuff.

And the ultimate true cliché? They have more fun with the box. And there were always lots of 'free' nappy boxes.

Unwell

Despite my best efforts Small was, at times, unwell. No matter how I tried to avoid it, he came into contact with germs and bugs. I soon realised there was nothing I could do about it and there was nothing wrong with it. I hadn't done anything bad and ultimately it was necessary to build his immune system.

In the early days, at the first sign of illness I found myself at the doctor's surgery being reassured that there was nothing cataclysmically wrong. Slowly I learnt what needed attention and what didn't but it was always better to be sure.

When Small reached the age of 2 months I discovered the parents' number one friend, Calpol (Tylenol in the US), a liquid form of paracetamol (acetaminophen in the US). Other brands and own brands are available but, in the UK at least, Calpol has become a term used to describe liquid paracetamol generally, like Hoover for vacuum cleaner. Mention Calpol to any UK parent and they will smile.

Calpol was wonderful. If Small had any kind of illness Calpol seemed to help: fevers, reduced; headaches, banished; aches and pains, gone; teething pain, eradicated. The added benefit was that Small often fell asleep after a dose of Calpol. That didn't mean I could use it as a sleeping aid. Not only would that have been potentially dangerous, it would not have worked. There was nothing sleep inducing in Calpol, it was just that once Small's pain and discomfort had been relieved, he could relax and catch up on the sleep it had been keeping at bay.

My first contact with Calpol was after Small's first set of immunisations. In the UK Smalls are immunised against all sorts of nasties that nowadays seem like small matters but in the past have been major killers (and still are in undeveloped countries). They only seem like small matters because they are such rare occurrences thanks to the immunisations. When Small 1 was born there was considerable news coverage about, now discredited, research linking the MMR vaccine for Measles, Mumps and Rubella to bowel disease and autism. Many parents refused the vaccine and as a result, there have been later outbreaks of the diseases with some fatalities.

The immunisation worked by giving Small a micro dose of the disease, which his immune system could cope with. His immune system then learnt how to deal with the disease so if it was attacked again it could fend it off. The immediate upshot was that Small felt unwell and became slightly feverish and Calpol was recommended to tackle the symptoms.

The immunisations themselves were harrowing for both of us. As house husband, the task of taking Small to the doctors landed on my shoulders. First immunisations take place at 2 months and at that stage Small had not suffered any injury. There were no bumps, bruises or cuts of any kind to mar Small's perfect form. That was all to come later, once he could move about. Other than wind or being hungry or too hot or cold, Small had never experienced any real trauma. That was about to change and I had to witness it and, worse, take a part in it.

Immunisations come in the form of an injection. Personally I hate injections; I have a real phobia and can become faint at the mere thought. It is totally irrational, the pain is nothing much, but my body reacts and I have to lie down to take them. I don't even like watching someone else having them. So, I was not the best choice as the person required to proffer Small's naked chubby thigh to the hypodermic wielding nurse.

To distract both Small and myself from the needle puncturing the perfection of his flesh I talked to him and kept eye contact. As the needle breached his skin his brow puckered. As the plunger was pressed and the micro toxins seeped into his bloodstream his eyes narrowed, fixing me with an accusing stare. There was pain and I was holding him. More accusing than the stare were the tears welling in the corners of his eyes. In counterpoint, when the needle was extracted the first drop of blood to escape Small's inside welled up from the tiny hole left by the incursion into his flesh.

It was a horrible, traumatic experience for both Small and me but thankfully it was over.

"Just hold the other leg now please," said the nurse, reaching for a second hypodermic.

Small knew what was coming this time and at the first scratch to his flesh he started to scream and my heart screamed along with him. After the evil deed I cuddled him close and his tears had subsided even before we reached the door, which wasn't long; we were both in escape mode. But the deed was done. I dosed him with Calpol and he slept like a baby: not very well and with lots of loud interruptions necessitating cuddles and rocking.

There were more immunisations at 3 months, 4 months and 12 months. Each of these involved double screaming because he knew what was coming the moment his chubby thighs were exposed. But better a few minutes of pain and screaming than the potential of days of suffering from any of the diseases immunised against and their potential long term effects.

Vomiting

Remember that scene in the exorcist with the green projectile vomiting? Well, that was based on Small. [Not the rotating head though.]

Walking

I like walking. I will happily walk for miles and miles. I particularly like walking on Dartmoor, where I can pretty much spin on the spot, point in any direction and then walk that way for hours without having to worry about the bother of crossing private land. What I hadn't realised, until I had Small as a walking companion, was that I always walked with a purpose. That purpose might vary, say, to walk a certain distance or to reach a specific destination, but there would invariably *be* a purpose.

Small, on the other hand, had the same attitude to walking as the doidens (see Doidens) did; there was no purpose in the walk itself, other than to take him from one interesting thing to another. Arguably, I was doing the same thing, it was just that the things I found interesting were quite different to Small (and the doidens). I, for instance, had very little interest in horse poo, other than to avoid stepping in it. Small and the doidens loved it. The doidens liked to eat it and roll in it. Small liked to carry it around by the armful. Other things of interest included stones, dead and rotting leaves, mud, any other kind of animal poo and sticks (although many adult males retain the pre-programmed instinct to carry a stick on a walk and have impulses to thrust and parry at any dodgy looking bushes).

Small was not content carrying one or two of these things. He would keep picking them up until his arms were full and then start loading them onto me. Woe betide me if I couldn't carry them all. Sometimes I could cast some of them away a few minutes after they had been passed to me but if I tried it with any unusual looking items it would be noticed and I had to go back and find them. The collection of interesting things would be carried to the end of the walk and would have to be placed reverently in the boot of the car, where hopefully it would be forgotten about and could be disposed of later. For the times that the collection was not forgotten by the time we arrived home, I had to instil in Small an understanding that collections of sticks, stones, rotting leaves and poo were best kept by the front door, not inside the house. Even though our smallest Small is not really small anymore we still have a collection of sticks and rocks by the front door (the rotting leaves and poo having long since decomposed).

Whilst Small shared an affinity for sticks and poo with the doidens, he lacked their rudimentary framework of obedience and loyalty. When the doidens stopped to sniff and explore everything within a hundred metre radius of the path they would eventually catch up if I carried on walking. Small did not have this ability, perhaps because he was slightly less intelligent and unable to grasp the concept or, conversely, that he was far more intelligent (and certainly more cunning and wily) and knew that if he didn't follow me then I would eventually have to turn around and come back to him. As a result, whilst walks of miles and miles still existed, I didn't actually travel very far. To illustrate, if I walk with my doidens they will invariably walk and run three times further than me as they chase hither and thither, back and forth, yet at the same time generally move in the same direction as me, at the same aggregate speed. With Small it was me that had to walk three times further, backwards and forwards along the path, desperately trying to get him to travel in the required direction. In fact, if I plotted my movement and his I am convinced that, on average, he would have been travelling in completely the opposite direction to me most of the time. The only time he would have been travelling in the required direction (please note that this was my required direction, not his) was when, in a desperate effort to make some progress, he had have been hoisted up and carried for a hundred metres (only to wander back seventy when he was put down).

Life had been much easier when Small was Really Small and strapped to my back. Except when he was pulling my ears or wiping sticky hands in my hair. Oh, and don't let Really Small carry a stick.

When Small first mastered walking he wanted to do it all the time. I could not stop him. He also tried to get to running far sooner than he should have done. Downhills were the places to be most alert. Small had not worked out his brakes and just got faster and faster down the slope until his legs couldn't keep up with his body and he crashed. If I hadn't managed to catch him there would be lots of tears but not much learning, at least on his behalf.

Once Small had conquered walking and running and braking he gave it all up. Having sorted the mobility thing out he no longer wanted to do it. He would constantly want to be back in the pushchair or carried. He would collapse to the ground declaring, "I can't walk, I've got bendy legs!"

Xylophone

Every family with a Small will probably have a collection of xylophones, drums, castanets, cymbals, trumpets, whistles and other 'musical' instruments. All unsuspecting, the parents will have bought one of these items and then been driven crazy within a minute. The rest will be presents from well-meaning or vindictive friends and relatives.

Small was once given a very loud toy electric guitar on a visit to relatives. It was handed over just before we all crammed into the car for the drive home. The relatives waved cheerily as we set off for a four hour journey from hell. We had the unenviable choice between loud, crashing, discordant guitar noises or loud, crashing, distraught Small noises filling the tiny, inescapable space we were hurtling down the road far too fast in, trying to make the experience as short as possible.

The thing was, Small and xylophones (or cacophonic noise making equivalents) were extremely compatible. Small loved his noise makers and wanted to demonstrate his skills at every moment. Sadly, Small and xylophones AND his parents were completely incompatible. There is a box in the loft, well buried in case of Small incursion, containing all of the loving gifts we ever received.

You Time

This was escape time; got to get out of here before I go mad, time. It was vital to take the mental weight off from time to time. It was not necessarily a great weight but it was there 24/7, inexorably dragging me down.

My escape was a ride on my bicycle. In the early days of Small that meant an hour grabbed at the weekend. Once I had trained up the secondary carer to a sufficient degree that she was confident to cope with Small alone for long enough, I could occasionally sneak off for a whole day!

Your Perfect Small

Your Small is perfect. So is everyone else's. We all live in a bubble. It is best to understand this. Nobody will see their child as the brat they really are and you will not win any Noble Peace Prizes by pointing this out.

ZZZZ (Lack of)

We all know what sleep deprivation can feel like. It is not nice.

The thing is, in the past, the causes had been pleasurable. I knew that if I was going on a weekend-long bender I was going to feel crap on Monday morning but could balance that against the good time preceding it. Weighing the two together the good time won.

Not being able to afford a live-in carer to deal with all the night interruptions, once Small was on the scene sleep deprivation was unavoidable. Night after night of interrupted sleep for week after week was way too high a price to pay for a fleeting, fumbled few minutes of pleasure several months previously. The balance was all wrong.

In the first few days I survived on adrenaline but that soon wore off. For the next few weeks (possibly months, it was all a blur) I was ready to sleep just about anywhere at any time and if I could, I did.

Of course, having a Small and being sleep deprived is one of the biggest clichés going. And whilst there were plenty of people ready to take a jab at my expense I had to accept that it was a reality. I just had to live through it and hold to the fact that at some point things would get better. Wouldn't they?

Here are some of the symptoms I suffered from whilst seriously sleep deprived:

- Going out and leaving the front door wide open.
- Putting the milk in the cupboard and the coffee jar in the fridge.
- Shutting my head in the cupboard.
- Not noticing the above.
- Not noticing the above and slamming the door a couple of times wondering what was jamming it.
- Beeping a trolley load of shopping through the till at the supermarket and then realising I didn't have my wallet.
- Forgetting to pick Small up from crèche.
- Having a terrible short term memory (really short – a matter

of seconds).

- Getting everyone's names wrong or not remembering them at all – even my wife's!
- Being clumsy, dropping everything I touched.
- Getting emotional.
- Suffering from continuous colds.
- Being unable to make simple decisions/process ideas.
- Having difficulty focusing, physically and mentally.
- Getting in the back seat of the car and wondering where the steering wheel had gone.
- Never being able to finish a

Funnily enough, if I listed the signs of getting older it would be very similar. Perhaps I just got old during that fuzzy period of my life when Small first arrived? It certainly feels that way.

Final Words

During my days as a house husband I received a considerable amount of advice on parenting. Nearly all of it came from unqualified sources and most of that was entirely unsolicited.

When I became a parent I must have developed a magic aura, a field of force that attracted possibly well-meaning people and invited them to offer me advice that I didn't want. Everyone had some tip to offer or some painful anecdote to recite. Most came from people that had been through the minefield of Small raising and were safe on the other side. Those I could tolerate to some degree. It was the advice from those whose only experience of Smalls was vicarious that annoyed me the most, especially when they were firing off tired old clichés that they had picked up conversationally with no experience of the reality of raising Smalls. As I picked my path between the mines, half by cautious testing and half by blind luck, these clichéd remarks were not helpful and were certainly not appreciated.

The ones that grated on my nerve endings the most were:

- It's just a phase;
- They change your life;
- You've got your hands full;
- You'll look back on this and laugh; and my particular favourite
- Enjoy every minute, they'll be grown up before you know it!

Well:

- It might be a phase but I've still got to deal with it now;
- Yes, my life is over;
- Well, nah! Stop stating the bloody obvious and open the door for me!;
- I'm already laughing! Can't you hear me!! Ha!!! Ha ha ha!!! Ha ha ha ha ha!!!!!; and
- It can't happen soon enough!

I suppose that, "It's just a phase," was meant sympathetically, reminding me that the latest Small issue would not last forever. On one level I could see that. I knew Small was not going to be crawling into my bed every night because he was scared of the monsters in the cupboard when he was 16 (at least I hoped not) but right then I was finding it very hard to visualise on that level because my sleep deprived mind couldn't focus beyond the moment.

At least, "It's just a phase," had a positive meaning, unlike its close cousin, "If you think this is bad, wait until…" Such as, "If you think he's a handful now, wait until he starts crawling!" [Where have I heard that before?] This was the same as saying, "It's just a phase and it's nowhere near as bad as the next one is going to be so get over yourself." Look, I was having a tough time right then. I didn't need to know it was going to get worse. I'd cross that bridge when I came to it. [I'm using clichés now.]

The truth was, my life *had* changed, mainly because I *did* have my hands full all the time. I *had* lived through some of the phases and *could* look back and laugh, sometimes without that brittle edge of hysteria. But I had not enjoyed every minute. I would be lying if I said I had, especially in the early days. I was a mindless, shambling, semi-automated version of my former self, functioning on terror induced adrenaline. Every cry, sneeze and rash had me reaching for the keypad or the phone. I had no time to myself and everything took twice as long as it used to. Leaving the house became a military style operation, requiring precise timing and a back breaking load of equipment to ensure survival in hostile territory. Things were bleak and the immediate future looked bleaker still for there was no sign of improvement on the horizon and I could only get more tired as time went on.

Then, on the point of breaking down in despair Small dragged me into the sunlight. He reached out and grabbed my finger and I knew what it was all about.

Since then I have discovered that there is no fail-safe route through the minefield. No amount of well-intentioned advice from other people provides a clear map; most of the way has to be plotted by gut instinct and trial and error. I have learnt alongside Small and we have both grown.

And when everything seems to be going bottom shaped [a mixed metaphor of bottom up and pear shaped] and everyone else seems to be so much better at it than me I just remind myself that they are not, they are just better at camouflage.